72STEPS

72 STEPS

by Karen Sloan-Brown

BROWN REFLECTIONS

72 Steps

Copyright © 2014 by Karen Sloan-Brown

All rights reserved.

No part of this work may be reproduced or transmitted in any form or by any means, electronic or mechanical, including photocopying and recording, or by any information storage or retrieval system, except as may be expressly permitted by the 1976 Copyright Act or in writing from the publisher. Requests for permission should be addressed to Brown-Reflections.com or Karensloanbrown.com.

This book is printed on acid-free paper.

ISBN: 978-0-9915517-8-1
Library of Congress Cataloging-in-Publication Data on file.

Editor: Cornelius Brown

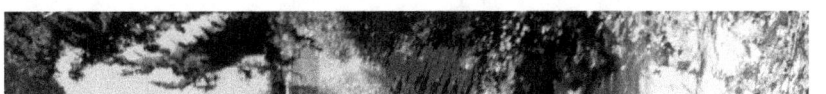

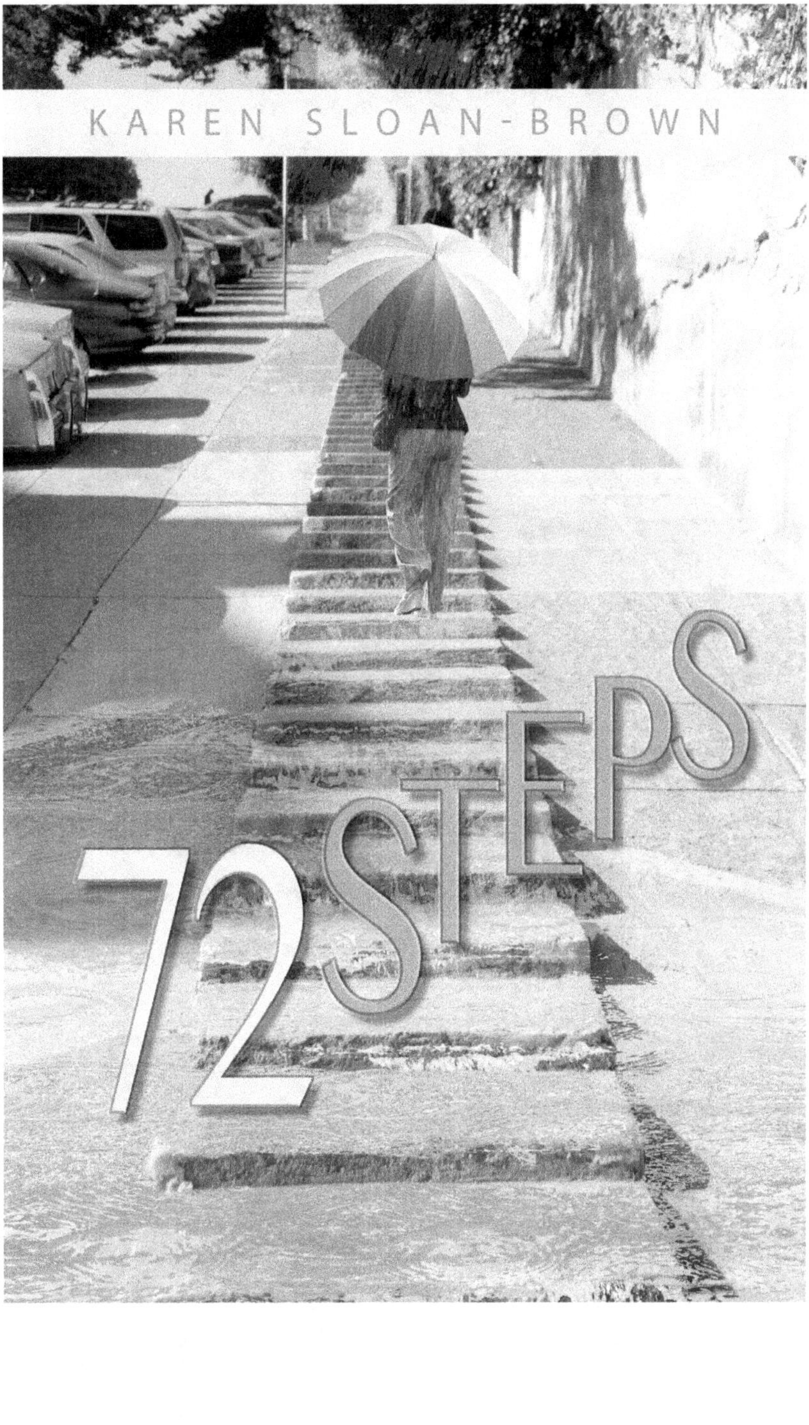

Dedication

This book is dedicated to my Lord and Savior, Jesus Christ. I acknowledge him in all His ways and thank Him for all that He has brought me through. I thank Him for my husband, my children, my mother, my father, my sisters and brothers, and all my extended family. I thank him for all the friends that he has brought into my life, all the teachers that have taught me, all the challenges that have influenced me. I thank Him for the path that he set before me, for carrying me, keeping me, and leading me. I thank my Heavenly Father, for His mercy and His grace. You are my source of strength and the love that sustains me. I thank my father, Rev. Cordell Holland Sloan, for showing me how to persevere.

Chapter One

The Unexpected

This is a story of inspiration, a rebirth of spirit, of survival, and of miracles. Where does it begin? It began at a similar point for all stories of triumph and overcoming the odds, at the lowest point in a life. It's the point where we either choose to start living or to start dying. Unlike watching a feature film there was no dramatic music building to a crescendo to denote the oncoming disaster or enemy. There was no warning of impending danger, no signs or premonitions that would foretell how drastically our lives were about to change.

Certainly life presents us all with an abundance of unexpected occurrences and fortunately most are glancing blows from which we quickly recover. I had experienced my own personal set of challenges with many up and downs but nothing I couldn't handle or that the Lord hadn't stepped in right on time to save me. I could never have imagined how completely my world would be rocked to its very core.

My name is Karen Sloan-Brown and my story begins in 2001, my husband's name is Cornelius Brown. We have three daughters, Courtney, 14, Kim, 9, and Casey, almost 2 years old, and we lived in Nashville, Tennessee. It was springtime, one of the most beautiful seasons of the year as nature was in full bloom showing off all her grandeur in the brightest skies and the most colorful of flowers. It was the beginning of May, which was a busy month for our family with Casey's birthday, the youngest of my three daughters, Mother's day, and the ending of the school year.

Unknowingly the storm began on Wednesday, May 2, 2001. Our schedule had gone as usual. Cornelius dropped Courtney off at school before work. I dropped Casey at the Born Again Day Care Center, and then Kim at Hull Jackson before heading to work.

I was a senior research assistant working for a medical research fellow at Meharry Medical College, but his lab was still temporarily located on Vanderbilt University Medical Center's campus. I went through the maneuverings and experiments of a regular day. After work I picked up the kids in reverse. Nothing was out of the ordinary, except Courtney didn't feel well. She was complaining of a headache and an upset stomach. With three children it wasn't really unusual for somebody to be out of sorts. "She's probably got some virus," I said to myself, most of the time they don't last for more than a day or two. I prayed it was a twenty-four hour virus and nobody else would catch it. We got through dinner and I found some moments to relax and unwind before the preparations of another day.

Cornelius was working two jobs at the time, days at Nashville Electric Service Company changing out and disconnecting meters and driving for Metropolitan Transit Authority for eight hours in the evening. We usually got to spend a few minutes with him in the morning before he and Courtney left for school and work, and I tried my best to wait up for him in the night. He usually got home after midnight around 12:30.

The next morning, Courtney still wasn't feeling up to snuff so I told her to just stay home for a day. I dressed and went through the normal routine to get everyone out to their designated places. I don't remember the details of that Thursday except for when I looked in on Courtney in her room that evening when I got home from work. She was getting up from the floor and I was stopped in my tracks by the color of her skin, her face looked ashen and gray. I had never seen anything like that before, her face was drained of any color. I became very worried, something wasn't right. I told her that I was taking her to the doctor first thing in the morning.

I didn't mention anything about it to Cornelius that night. He was always working so hard and I tried not to worry him unless it was necessary. We had a high overhead having built our dream home some seven years ago and our finances were stressed with the problems of renters at our old house. Cornelius was always on the moody side so I tried to keep stress levels down by holding a tight rein on the girls and running the house while he focused his energies on working.

First I took Casey to the daycare and then dropped Kim at school, and quickly returned home to take Courtney to the pediatric clinic. It then occurred to me that I should call the doctor's office first to make sure that they could fit us in that morning. In my anxiousness I hadn't even thought about an appointment.

"It's not booked heavy today, just bring her right in" the receptionist said, and I began to feel relieved, at least that wouldn't be a problem. It was after the morning rush hour so I made the drive in good time as my eyes drifted to the rearview mirror to look at Courtney whenever I felt I could. By the time I pulled into the clinic parking lot, Courtney was even more out of it than when we left the house as she struggled to hold her eyes open. While we walked in I noticed she was still wearing the clothes she'd slept in the night before. Holding the door for her as we walked inside, I could see there wasn't anyone else in the outer office. Courtney found a chair while I signed her name on the patients' clipboard and then I sat down next to her.

We were sitting in the waiting room for about 10 minutes when Courtney said, "Mama, tell them I need a CAT-scan."

The words stunned me and made my stomach flutter nervously. Why would she say such a thing and what does she know about a CAT-scan. I tried to distract myself by looking at magazines between mental critiques of the décor and how well the wall color went with the carpet and chairs.

After a short time the black nurse that assisted Dr. Ryan took us back to the examining room. It occurred to me as she took Courtney's vital signs that for the many times we had met I didn't know her name. I guess people try to stay detached and impersonal in the doctor's office. When Dr. Ryan, a short pixie type of a woman who reminded me of a female Peter Pan with glasses, came into the examining room she asked us what was going on and what her symptoms were and how long had it been. I told her that Courtney had come home from school sick and that she had been complaining about a headache, that she was very nauseated, and that she felt she needed a CAT-scan.

Dr. Ryan looked into her eyes, ears and throat, listened to her heart and lungs as I watched. After her examination Dr. Ryan said that she couldn't find anything right off, it was nothing neurological, but that Courtney was very dehydrated. She had the nurse bring us some Gatorade and water, but even with small sips she couldn't keep it down and kept complaining of a terrible headache. The nurse gave her a couple of Tylenols for the pain, but they didn't help much.

After about twenty minutes the nurse poked her head into the examining room later saying she would be right back to hook up an IV so they could give Courtney some fluids for her dehydration. It wasn't long before she wheeled in the thin sliver pole along with a monitor and the clear bag of fluid in her other hand. As I watched the nurse touching and massaging Courtney's hands looking for the best vein to insert the IV, I noticed that Courtney had drawn the words, 'Courtney and Ronnie', and 'Courtney Yates' on her hand in green marker. It took my thoughts back to a few weeks ago when I picked her and Kim up from children's choir rehearsal at church.

She had gotten into the car so excited and smiling, saying, "Mama I have something to tell you."

"What is it I," asked her?

"I'm in a relationship," she proudly exclaimed.

I just smiled to myself.

"You're not in a relationship," I replied. "What are you talking about girl?"

"I am, Mama, Ronnie and I go together."

I looked at her in the rearview to see her expression. I thought how cute she was as she beamed with excitement. It was a sweet moment seeing my oldest having the new experience of liking a boy. She had worn her favorite outfit to choir rehearsal because he was going to be there. Her red bandana tied in the back with her hair hanging straight down in the back, her Eddie George Titan football jersey, her Calvin Klein cropped jeans with a cuff, and her Tommy Hilfiger sneakers. She talked all the way home about what he said and then what she said as she bubbled over and I tried to pretend that I wasn't touched by it and proud that she had shared it with me.

I watched the nurse stick the needle for the IV in a vein next to the words 'Courtney and Ronnie' written on her hand. Then I looked up at Courtney's face for the great reaction, but she didn't even flinch. That's when I really knew she was not herself and was totally out it. She could never stand needles. Even as a toddler she would not cooperate when it was time to take her shots, not until the whole office staff and I were covered in perspiration.

I clearly remember pulling a muscle in my back when she was five, trying to hold her still so her previous pediatrician could give her one of her scheduled boosters. She struggled so hard as I tried to loop my legs around hers as she strained her little body to break free. It took all the energy of both the doctor and me to get through the drama of those shots. When we got home, I told Cornelius that was my last time taking her to get any more shots; he was definitely on duty for the next one.

To see Courtney not even raise her head I knew something was very wrong. It took several hours for the IV drip to finish and she slept most of the time. As I sat there and looked at her hair, her skin, the muscles in her arms, I thought about the miracle of birth, how another human being is created within another. How this child was my own flesh and blood. She was me, only better. She was smart like me, but she was more confident. She looked like me, but she was prettier. I was shy, but she strutted around with her head held high like she was royalty. She wanted to go to law school like I did when I was young, but I didn't have the fortitude to push toward the dream and I knew she could do anything she set her mind to. We're both independent though and we talked about her wanting to go to college in New York or either California.

We finally left the doctor's office around 5:00 that evening. It had taken all day to get enough fluids into her system, but she seemed to feel better and her color was much improved. I began to feel reassured and glad that I had brought her in and I could tell that Courtney was glad we had come also. We picked up Kim and Casey on the way home and I put some food from the fridge together to make a meal. I called Cornelius on the phone later and told him what had happened at the doctor.

"It's good that you took her", he said, "Let me speak to her."

They talked for just a minute, but he got her to smile. That girl was a "no doubt about it" Daddy's girl.

Dr. Ryan called the next morning to check on Courtney. I told her she was a little better but she still didn't have much energy. She advised us to make sure that we had Courtney to drink plenty of fluids all through the day and eat a bland diet.

***

Saturday mornings were the busiest time at our house. There were chores and laundry to be done. Plus, having a two year old around kept us all occupied. After getting her cleaned up and changed in the morning, Casey would run straight into her sisters' room and do her Superman dive on top of Courtney. I don't know why or when it started, but Courtney had made a pallet on the floor between her bed and the wall and she preferred to sleep there rather than in her bed. Casey would love to wake her up, and sit on her, lay on her; she just wanted to be close to her. Kim was always a little jealous that Casey gravitated to Courtney, but Courtney just gave off warmth, a protective vibe that always drew other kids to her.

This Saturday was a sneaker day. Everything we did was a family project, which was just a thing with Cornelius. On the weekend, whatever was going to be done, we all had to participate. When we got to Rivergate, we fanned out into the Shoe Carnival Store to look for our shoe of choice among the wall displays. Cornelius and I were partial to New Balance at the time and Courtney and Kim wanted to get Saucony's. Courtney's energy seemed to be fading quickly as we shopped so I thought we'd stop at Kroger's on the way home to get some ice cream. I thought the sugar and extra calories might give her a boost. She had gotten pretty tired in the Shoe Carnival and wanted to sit in the car and wait for us but Cornelius insisted that she come in. After all we had to do everything together. She dragged her feet slowly down the aisles while we shopped but she made it.

We all dove into the ice cream as soon as we got home, but Courtney couldn't keep hers down. I thought maybe we needed to stay with the fluids and bland diet until her stomach virus settled down. She was miserable and slept for most of the weekend. I gave her Advil for her headache and tried to get her to eat some boiled rice, but she didn't have an appetite and could take only a few small forkfuls at a time.

Courtney felt a bit better on Monday morning, at least she was rested. I encouraged her to try and make it to school since it was close to the end of the year. I didn't want her to miss much before final exams so that she could keep her grades up. She had already gotten the letter notifying her that she would be attending J.T. Creswell High School, a couple of months earlier. We had gone to the new school and chosen her classes for her freshman year in high school. She was excited about it and I could see that my 'big girl' was growing up.

That morning Cornelius dropped her off at school and I went through the rituals of an otherwise normal day. Shortly after lunch I received a phone call from the school that Courtney was feeling sick and needed to be picked up. I quickly wrapped up whatever I was working on and headed over to the school. I went into the office to let them know I was there and stood outside in the hallway to wait for her to come down. I couldn't believe my eyes when I saw her being brought down the stairs with her teacher on one side and her best friend Kenya holding her up on the other side. Her hair was mussed and her skin looked ashen to me again.

Her eyes were practically closed as I rushed over and tried to support her weight on my hip while she leaned against it. As we stumbled to the car I wondered what had made her feel this bad so quickly from this morning. I called the doctor back as soon as we got inside the door at home. Dr. Ryan said the headaches and neck aches could be from her not eating, but not to worry so much about the eating; just make sure we kept up with the fluids. She mentioned that sometimes teenagers get depressed and behave this way. I knew that Courtney was not the type of child to get depressed but I was grasping for answers. She had never been a sickly child and seeing her feeling bad day after day was wearing on my nerves. After another day of watching her suffer in pain I asked Dr. Ryan for the referral to the center they had for troubled teenagers.

 The next week was tough. Casey's two-year birthday came and Courtney didn't feel up to going to her party. Then on Mother's Day she literally dragged herself to church. In the preparation of the morning I didn't notice what she was wearing. Glancing down the pew at her in church I could see she was still wearing the clothes she had been lounging around in the house and they were very wrinkled. What was going on I thought to myself, this wasn't like Courtney. She took a lot of care in her appearance. What's wrong with my child?

    We spent the next few days trying to get through. She would sleep most of the day and I was glad it gave her some relief from the headache. I made mixtures of boiled rice with a bit of chopped spinach trying to find something she could keep down. She would lay on the floor next to my feet and I would feed her tiny bites with only a few grains of rice, hopeful that any amount of food she took would give her some energy.

    There were times when I was worried and would walk in the bonus room to talk about it to Cornelius, only to find him starring helplessly out into space. He couldn't stand to see her going through this thing whatever it was, so I just pulled myself back together and went back to the den to be with Courtney. She didn't have much energy to go up and down the stairs so we sometimes spent the night downstairs. Kim and Casey slept in their beds, Courtney and me in the den, and Cornelius alone on the couch in the bonus room.

    By this time Courtney had already missed a week of school. I went by to speak with her teachers and pick up her assignments so she could keep up since it was close to the end of the school year. She would try so hard to do her homework assignments at the kitchen table but she was in so much pain she could barely keep her head up. She would do some and then would have to lie back down again in the den, and she always would rest on the floor, never on the couch.

    Cornelius seemed to stay out of the way when he wasn't working. I guess he didn't know what to do and he couldn't stand to see her hurting. One of my busy-body cousins who had never even come by to visit or talk to me called and said she thought that maybe Courtney had anorexia or an eating disorder. I told her I didn't think so but thanked her for calling.

    The Advil wasn't doing anything to relieve the headaches and Courtney complained that her neck was also hurting badly. I was feeling like we couldn't keep on like this, it was torture, so the next morning I took her back to the doctor. Dr. Ryan gave her another check-up, and then asked her to walk. I noticed she was limping. Dr. Ryan assured me again that it wasn't anything neurological that it was probably from her sleeping and lying around so much. She thought Courtney may be trying to get attention and suggested that we talk with someone at the mental health clinic. Courtney was happier and encouraged after the doctor's appointment and even wanted a milkshake on the way home.

We picked up Kim and Casey on our way to the house, but when we got there, she couldn't keep the milkshake down. We spent another miserable weekend. On that Sunday evening while I was ironing, she came into the room and sat down on the bed next to me.

"Mama I can't take it anymore," she told me. "I just want to walk in front of a truck and let it be over."

The words knocked the strength out of me. She was crying and I felt so helpless. I didn't know what to do or say, but I did my best to stand there and not let her know that I wanted to fall to the floor and cry with her. I couldn't stand to see her in pain without being able to do anything about it. I called my Aunt Lillie who we were both close to on the phone by the bed near us. She gave Courtney a pep talk and encouraged her as much as she could giving me a few moments to pull it back together.

The next day Dr Ryan's partner, Dr. Mace called the house and said don't worry about the referral, that Courtney had tested positive for Mononucleosis. I didn't know anything about mono, except that I had heard it was the kissing disease. I was just glad and relieved that they had finally found out what was wrong. I thought it was odd though, Courtney was only fourteen, and I didn't think she had been doing much kissing if any. I asked was there anything we could give for the pain or vomiting, but she said there was no treatment for mono, she just had to wait it out. I did some research of my own on mono and found that the symptoms didn't match, so I called Dr. Ryan to discuss it. She told me that Courtney had an atypical case.

It was Monday, May 21, 2001, and after another rough weekend, I noticed Courtney wasn't using her left arm. I knew then that something was really wrong and whatever it was it was getting worse. I took her hand, looked into her eyes and told her to wait for me, "I'm going to take Kim to school and Casey to the daycare and I'm coming right back to take you to the doctor."

When I got back she looked at me, gave me a relieved smile, and said, "I thought you weren't coming back."

I just sunk inside feeling for her and what she was going through.

"You know I was coming back for you, girl, don't be silly," I tried to say lightly as we got into the car.

I drove as quickly and as carefully as I could and found a parking space not far from the door. As we slowly walked into the clinic I noticed that she had on her house slippers and was wearing her Pisces sleep shirt with the tear in it. She didn't care and neither did I, we needed help. During the examination Dr. Mace asked her to face the wall and lift her arm and when she couldn't my heart began to break and my eyes filled with tears, tears I knew I couldn't let fall, so I blinked them back and tried to look calm when Courtney turned around.

Dr. Mace left the room after the examination and when she returned she told me that she had ordered a CAT-scan and we were to wait for a hospital transport person to come for us. The hospital transport employee was a woman I had seen around the VUMC campus many times over the years when I went to the hospital cafeteria for lunch. She got Courtney strapped into the wheel chair and I followed her. Walking behind them my mind seemed to be racing so fast that I couldn't think or maybe the fear of the unknown was beginning to set in.

When we got to the area where the CAT-scans were done,

they wheeled her in and I waited outside. I waited for what seemed like an hour before I was told that she would be admitted into the hospital. They wheeled Courtney up to the pediatric floor of the hospital and a nurse helped her get settled in the room and into the bed. A few minutes later two doctors came in and introduced themselves but I don't remember their names. One of them told me that they had discovered a brain tumor about the size of a lemon on the right rear side of her head. They told me that a neurosurgeon would be around later to talk to me about the surgery and then they left.

Courtney looked confused at first and then she reached for me.

"Mama, they said I have a brain tumor," she said with fear in her eyes.

"Don't worry," I told her, holding her hands in mine. "Everything is going to get better now that we know what is wrong."

I told her about my Dad having a brain tumor when he was a around her age. I told her that he had his surgery and went on with the rest of his life. The story seemed to calm both of us down as we recovered from the shock of the morning. While she rested I called Cornelius and told him everything the doctors told us. He said he would pick up Kim and Casey and take them to my Mother's and get there as soon as he could.

The medications they had given Courtney allowed her to get some much need rest and relief. While I waited in her room a nurse came in and gave me some information off the Web about pediatric brain tumors. I was stunned as I sat there and read the list of symptoms, my child had every one of them from the first day we went to see Dr. Ryan, headache, nausea, vomiting, fatigue, and weakness, all I could do was shake my head in anger and frustration.

Cornelius had just arrived at the hospital before the surgeon for Courtney came into the room and introduced himself. He told us with confidence that he had done this surgery several times before.

"It's usually a benign tumor," he said without concern, "The recovery time is around two months and children go back to living their lives."

He talked about a case he had just done on a five year old girl. He was very reassuring and casual. He mentioned that they had scheduled her surgery for the following week, after Memorial Day. Unfortunately they were booked until then. It would be a week before her operation. When I think about this experience I am amazed at how impersonal the process of someone operating on your body is. There is no relationship with this individual that you are trusting enough to put your life or the life of a member of your family in their hands.

After the doctor left, Courtney turned to me a little afraid and upset and asked, "Mama, am I going to be OK?"

Cornelius was devastated. He couldn't stand to hear her upset like that. He moved across the room to the far wall and leaned against it and covered his face. I was shaken. I had never seen this man cry or show any emotion in the 20 years that we had been together.

I grabbed Courtney's hand and squeezed it, and I told her, "Don't you worry until you see me worry. You are going to be fine." I told them the whole story of how my Dad had a brain tumor when he was twelve, and how much he suffered because of segregation in hospitals at the time. I kept talking about how no one wanted to operate on him because he was black, and how finally someone showed some human kindness and did the surgery. It turned out the tumor was benign and he was fine afterwards.

When Courtney was given some medications that stopped the pain her appetite returned and we felt like we were at least moving in the right direction. It was good to see her eat without throwing it back up. She seemed to have gathered her emotions and fears, at least on the surface, and Cornelius and I followed her lead. We decided to take turns staying with her at the hospital overnight. Cornelius had filed the papers at his job to take family leave until Courtney got better; he wanted to be there for her through the whole ordeal.

In the evenings, she wanted to watch comedies, things that made her laugh and kept her mind off of everything. Her favorite movie was *The Nutty Professor*, and we'd watch it over and over. We'd rent other movies to watch and stay up late into the night. One night the video store had just closed in Kroger's when we got there. I pleaded with the guy there through the closed gate to please let me rent *The Klumps* for my daughter who was in the hospital and he opened the door and let us in. We were so thankful. It was one of those times that a little thing meant so much.

One day during the week Ronnie's parents brought him to the hospital to visit Courtney and it made her day. It surprised me when Cornelius said we should go out of the room and leave them some time to visit alone. We spoke to his parents in the waiting room. Ronnie's father was the choir director for the children's choir so he was concerned about her and said he would pray for us. His mom, Sherry, said that Ronnie really wanted to come to the hospital so they thought they should bring him. She also mentioned that he had asked them if he could take her to the movies, but they hadn't had the chance to arrange it yet. I thanked them for taking the time to bring him to the hospital. It seemed to raise her spirits whenever friends came.

Another night we were sitting up talking and she said her name out loud.

"Courtney Nicole Brown, I like my name, Mama," she said.

"I like it too," I told her.

We sat a little longer and watched some romance show about a couple having problems on the LifeTime Channel and Smokey Robinson's song came on.

She laughed and asked, "Mama, do you think I ought to shop around?"

I laughed too and said, "Yes, I think you should."

Cornelius spent the next night at the hospital. At home I lay awake in the bed trying not to worry between my prayers for the Lord to heal her. I remembered a conversation I had with my dad when I was around Courtney's age. He had gone through a traumatic surgery to remove a large tumor from his pancreas. Nearly a third of his stomach had been removed and he was in constant pain. My dad was such a phenomenal human being and I hated to see him suffer every day.

"I don't think it's fair that you had to get sick," I told him.

"I would rather it happen to me than for any of you children to get sick," he said.

I now had a full understanding of what he told me that day, because I knew that Cornelius and I would have gladly traded places with our baby to spare her of this sickness. Seeing her go through this crisis was devastating.

I felt tired like I was in a daze the next morning. After dropping Casey at the daycare and on my way to Kim's school I realized that the school years was about to end. I needed to sign Kim up for her summer program. I stopped by Fisk to pick up the paper work for Mini-College. I had spoken with Roberto, my boss, about what was going on with my family and he told me not to worry about coming into the lab until we got Courtney home.

I drove on to the hospital and when I walked into Courtney's room she was in good spirits, she saw me and her eyes brightened and she smiled.

"Look at you, Mama, trying to look cute," she said.

I smiled back and said, "Who told you I'm not cute?"

The steroids they were giving her were really increasing her appetite, so she sent me to the cafeteria to get her some more breakfast. Courtney was always partial to breakfast food.

We'd take her to Shoney's for the breakfast buffet on Saturday mornings quite often, and whenever we traveled we would stay at Embassy Suites where they would have the nice hot breakfast. She loved eggs and the grits, and now she was having this thing for Rice Krispies.

As I walked to the hospital cafeteria, I remember trying to see my reflection in the hospital window while I walked, trying to see what she saw when she looked at me. From what I could tell, I didn't look any different. Cornelius mentioned later that they had watched the movie, *A Perfect Storm*, and it had a sad ending, and he felt kind of bad about bringing it. I just rubbed his shoulders and told him not to worry about it.

Courtney was doing her part trying to keep her spirits up, and that meant a daily dose of *The Nutty Professor*, or the sequel. We would talk about different things and whenever she would worry I would tell her "All is well," and we would start saying it together. It was something I remember my Dad telling us whenever we were worried. That morning I helped her brush her teeth because her left side was getting weaker and I helped her take a shower. She thanked me with such a depth of sincerity that tore at my heart.

"I would do anything for you, baby," I told her. "I want to do these things and I wish I could do more. You don't have to thank me."

One particular time she was getting up to use the restroom. I knew that going to the bathroom was a struggle for her so I told her she didn't have to get up. She could just use the bedpan.

She smiled and said, "Mama. I'm trying to hold on to my pride and dignity."

"Okay, okay," I said jokingly, but she had touched my soul with those words.

Cornelius brought Kim and Casey to the hospital to visit after the last day of school. Courtney was so happy to see them. She called out their names loudly and held out her arms for hugs.

Kim was scared and a bit shocked to see Courtney in a wheel chair but Casey didn't notice and was glad to sit in her lap.

"Mama, make sure you take them to the doctor" she told me as she held Casey and Kim leaned against her wheelchair.

I watched them and thought about how well she took care of her younger sisters. I remembered Kim's first day at daycare, and how Courtney had come into the baby room with me. When I sat the baby carrier down on the floor to put Kim's things away in her cubbie, Courtney crouched down and covered the carrier with her body, and just rocked it. A curious little boy came over to try and look into the carrier and she shooed him away. The caregivers sensing my reluctance and Courtney's protectiveness were telling us she would be fine and not to worry. I looked at Courtney and her eyes were as full of tears as my own were. They had to promise to come and get her from her classroom later on in the day so she could check on Kim before she would finally leave. It had always been like that. If Kim fell off her bike, Courtney ran and got to her before I could. She was just as good with Casey as I was. She was the one who kept her calm on most of our driving trips.

On his way to the hospital, Cornelius had also picked up Courtney's report card and some medals she had won for an individual music competition she had participated in. She played the alto saxophone in the school band and was pretty good. We had all gone to see her in that competition about a month ago. I remember thinking how grownup she looked as she played that day, wearing a black skirt and a bright pink blouse and black heels. I also thought about how she played even though she had complained of a bad headache.

She was so happy and her smile reached from ear to ear when he told her that she had passed the eighth grade and was going to high school. Courtney had worried that missing the last weeks of school would have hurt her grades, but her teachers understood that she was sick and she had made good grades all year. She and her friend Kenya used to always talk about how they were going to college together far away from Nashville, California or New York, when they graduated from high school.

On Thursday, the doctors came in and said they were going to release her, saying she could go home for the weekend before her surgery. I was worried because her left side was so weak she could barely walk but I was glad she could come home. We would figure out how to manage when we got there. Cornelius went to pull the car around while I helped her get dressed. When the paper work was done I walked beside her with hospital transport pushing her in the wheelchair. On the drive home I sat in the back seat of the car with her just like I did after she was born. I watched her look out the window at things she had missed while she was in the hospital room.

My Mother was already at the house with the girls when we got there. They were just glad to see her back home. I cooked some things that I knew she liked and we relaxed and watched some TV. Cornelius and I were going to sleep downstairs with her instead of trying to carry her upstairs. She wanted to sleep on the floor as usual. I remember giving her some medication that the doctors had prescribed and for a minute she looked blank in her eyes and I thought she was choking, but before I could panic it passed.

The next morning when we woke she needed my help to get to the bathroom. While I was trying to support her and turn her towards the toilet she had a seizure. Her body stiffened and then seemed to collapse. I could barely hold her weight. It scared us so bad that we thought about calling an ambulance. Cornelius decided that we should drive her to emergency ourselves. He drove the car across the front yard as close to the front door as he could and we carried her to the car and drove her to Vanderbilt emergency.

After tests and MRI's they told us that the tumor had grown four centimeters since the last scans and that they were going to have to put in a drain to release some of the pressure that was causing the headaches and seizures to worsen. The doctors asked Cornelius and me to leave the room while they put the drain in and I wondered if it was because it was going to be very painful for her. We walked outside in silence along 21st Avenue and passed Pizza Perfect, one of the places we all liked to go for pizza. After about ten minutes we turned back around and returned to the room. I could see that they had shaved some of her hair off on the right side where the drain was put in.

We spent the rest of the long Memorial Day weekend back in the hospital. My family was very helpful in watching the girls and Courtney had lots of visits from family, friends, and our neighbors. The junior pastor at my church, Darryl Drumwright had come up to pray with us and Courtney was so happy about that. After he finished the prayer she smiled and said, "All is well."

Chapter Two

The Unknown

On the morning of her surgery on May 29, 2001, I prayed and asked the Lord to be the doctor's hand in the operating room. I prayed that the tumor was benign, and when I was finished I felt confident that God was with us and everything would be alright. Several of my aunts were there and they said that they had also prayed for Courtney and they just wanted us to know that they were there for us.

While we waited inside the pre-surgery area Courtney asked me again, "Mama, am I going to be okay?"

"I'm not worried at all," I told her, "God is with us and He has always taken care us. Don't worry until you see me worrying."

She talked about getting a job in the summer but I told her, "Child, you are not going to be working, you're just going to stay home with me and recuperate and get your strength back. We're going to spend the summer together."

Foolishly, I wasn't worried, I was nervous, but I had such faith. God had never let me down, and I felt favored that He would do what I asked. It had always been that way, even during the times when things looked hopeless.

A few family and friends came to say hello and give us some comforting words as we sat in the surgery waiting room. After a while the walls seemed to be closing in on us, so Cornelius and I went outside to get some air. As I watched people walking and talking, cars driving by, the traffic light changing colors, and students hanging out on the Peabody Campus across the street, I thought that it seemed like a normal day, but for us our world was in turmoil. My child lay inside that building on an operating table with her head cut open.

It couldn't be happening, what went wrong, what did we do wrong that would have caused her to have a tumor? Was it the fall where she bumped her head when she was learning to walk, was it from using the cordless phone, or sitting too close to the TV? My thoughts were jumbled and disconnected and screamed like a crazy woman inside my head. On the outside we both were quiet, unable to say much to each other, it was just too overwhelming. Just a few weeks ago everything seemed normal and now our baby was in there on an operating table with a brain tumor. There were no words.

We came back in after about an hour and set in the waiting room unaware of anyone else. A nurse came over to us and said Courtney was still in surgery but she was doing fine. Dr. Ryan stopped by the waiting room to ask us how things were going, but I couldn't stand to talk to her. I couldn't even look at her. When I thought about how much Courtney had suffered in those weeks because she couldn't see the symptoms starring her in the face during those doctor visits I wanted to ask her if she was stupid or just lacked common sense. Right or wrong I felt like she had caused my child unnecessary pain and I never wanted to see her again in my life.

The shock came after Courtney had been in surgery about four hours when a young doctor or intern came out and talked to us about the surgery. He told us that the tumor was malignant and my heart sank. He said they got out most of it but couldn't get all of it, that they would start her on chemotherapy as soon as possible. I couldn't even process that for a minute, what were they saying?

Then I began to talk to myself, gathering myself from the inside out, saying they don't know us, they don't know we won't be beat by this, they don't know our strength. I shifted into fight mode. I would do whatever I had to do to make sure she survived, it didn't matter, and I simply would not let her go. It wasn't much longer before they took us to the recovery room where we could see her. My strength that I had worked so hard to bring to the surface faltered when I saw her lying there in the bad with her head bandaged.

She looked like she had been through so much and we knew it wasn't over. How could I even tell her what the doctor had said to us about the tumor? I couldn't break her heart with that news, she had stayed so strong and hopeful through it all from the beginning. I called her name and she opened her eyes but was still very drowsy. She wanted to use the bathroom, but I told her she needed to use the bedpan. She had always refused to use it, but she didn't realize that she had just come out of surgery. That only seemed to upset her and she was getting more distressed because she didn't want to use the bedpan and she needed to go badly.

"Mama, I'm trying to hold on to my pride and my dignity," she told me with desperation rising in her voice.

She was a very proud girl, always had been. She walked liked it was her world, head and shoulders held high. I almost broke down because I didn't know what to do. Courtney began to have a seizure and the room filled with doctors or nurses, I don't know which. It seemed like we never saw the same person twice. Unfamiliar faces that said they were taking her down for a CAT-scan and a MRI.

My stomach was doing one flip after another and I thought I was going to be sick. They took us to this room to wait and I just began to pray. Cornelius and I didn't talk, we didn't know what to say, we were both in shock. It was about an hour later when a different doctor came into the room and told us that there had been a lot of blood in the surgery and the bleeding was causing the seizures. He said that they were giving her some medication to try and stop the bleeding. When he left the room my body began to tremble as if I were freezing cold. I tried to shake it off and another wave would come and start it all over again. I felt nauseated but I hadn't eaten in days.

We waited like that for about another hour when an older

doctor we had never seen before came into the room and said that Courtney had a large seizure where her brain had gone too long without oxygen and that there no waves showing. He told us she was on life support and we could decide what we wanted to do and if we wanted to donate her organs.

"What is he saying?" I asked myself.

He left the room, and I was speechless.

Cornelius started talking, "We're not going to let this devastate us and our family."

After that his voice trailed off into a fog. I don't know who we saw or who we talked to or what we said. We somehow went to our car and drove home.

"When I saw her after the surgery I knew she wasn't going to make it," Cornelius told me when we got home.

"I never thought that," I said quietly.

I couldn't believe that the Lord would let me down. We were special. We were survivors, nothing could beat us. I thought we had found favor with God. He had always blessed us. I thought we would win this battle too. We walked around in a daze for the rest of the day. I didn't know where Kim and Casey were or what they were doing the whole time or how they got home that afternoon. When Kim got home I brought her into the den to tell her what had happened. She and Courtney had always been so close I couldn't bear to tell her but I had no choice. I sat down close to her on the couch.

"Kim, Courtney had a seizure after the operation," I told her, "The doctors said that her brain had gone too long without oxygen. She won't be able to come home. She's gone to heaven."

"Mama," she cried out to me, "I didn't even get a chance to say goodbye."

She looked at me with such hurt in her eyes that I had to struggle not to break down.

"You can still say goodbye to her," I said. "You can go outside and tell her and she'll hear you."

I stood up and walked over to the French doors on the deck and opened the door for her. She stepped outside and I closed the door behind her. I watched from the inside as she began to talk. I couldn't hear what she was saying and I wished that I had gone out there with her, but I wanted her to be free to say what she wanted. Seeing her in pain talking to her big sister as she looked up to the clouds, I almost collapsed. Her hurt doubled my own hurt. I gathered myself as I saw her coming back to the door.

I gave her a big hug and told her, "We're going to be all right."

Later, Cornelius and I talked and decided to take Courtney off of life support the next day.

"She's was already gone," he said.

I called Pastor Drumwright and told him what had happened and what we were going to do in the morning. I didn't sleep much that night. I tried to keep still not to disturb Cornelius, although I think he was also awake.

The next day Cornelius didn't want to deal with taking Courtney off of the machines, he was angry and upset, he said he didn't want to go.

"The doctors don't need us there," he said sadly.

I knew we had to go but it wasn't an experience that any parent would ever want to go through. I sat on the side of the bed and wondered if I could do this without him. I knew he was feeling like I did, he didn't want this to be real. After a few minutes he began to get dressed and I followed. My mother went with us to the hospital and we were running behind schedule. As we were walking into the front we met Pastor Drumwright coming out. He turned around when he saw us coming and walked back in with us.

When we got inside Courtney's room there were several doctors and nurses already there. I felt as if everyone in the room was there to witness our misery, standing around watching our personal tragedy. I wanted them all to leave so we could be alone with her so I could talk and touch her in private, but I was frozen. I didn't ask for privacy and to this very day I still wish I had.

After a few moments one of the nurses asked, "Are you all ready?"

I nodded and said, "Yes."

The nurse walked over to the machines and monitors while we stood by the wall in front of the bed and began to turn off a number of switches. After she turned off the first one Cornelius gasped and turned his back as if he had been shot. When the nurse moved away from the bed I walked over to the bed and I touched Courtney's arm, except it didn't feel like hers. The warmth was gone. My eyes were drawn to the round circles of white tape with wires that monitored her vital signs and I gently tried to scratch one off without being seen. I wanted to rip all the tubes and wires off of her. I wanted her to be left alone. They had bothered her enough.

One doctor came over to us and quietly asked us if we wanted to donate her organs, Cornelius said no, and I was glad at the time, I didn't want them to touch her anymore. They gave us her belongings in a bag. Cornelius told the nurse he wanted the blanket that we had brought from the house to stay with her and then we walked out in silence. We dropped my mother off at home and then we went to the Wright Funeral Home to make arrangements.

Pastor Drumwright was already at the funeral home when we got there and that was a comfort to me. I didn't know how I could ever thank him for being there and going through this with us. My Aunt Hilda was also there and I didn't know how she knew we would be there but I was glad to see her. We were taken into a room and catalogs were spread across the table. The director started asking us about cars and flowers and items to go inside of a casket I didn't know what he was talking about but I gave him by best answers.

Cornelius took care of the details while I looked around

the room wondering how I got there. Through the window of the room I saw my brother Dell from California get out of a car. I didn't know how he had gotten to Nashville so fast, but I was glad he was there too. The funeral director then walked us into a room full of caskets. It was at this point that I became two people. One trapped in a horrible nightmare and the other one talking about what I wanted to buy for the funeral service. Courtney liked blue, so I picked out something pale blue. My voice seemed to fade out and I heard Cornelius talking before the volume of the voices around me were turned all the way down until all the arrangements were done and we were leaving.

There wasn't time to recover when we got home. As the day went on we were overwhelmed with family members coming to the house. My sisters and brothers from Philly and their kids had driven down and now it seemed to be so much noise, so much talking and laughing. I wondered why they had to stay with us. Why they couldn't just give us some peace and quiet. Cornelius went upstairs to our bedroom to rest for a while to get away from all the chaos. No one asked me what had happened or what I wanted, or what they could do. They just seemed to make themselves at home as if it were a family reunion. I stayed in the midst of the whirlwind for as long as I could and then I followed Cornelius upstairs to our bedroom and closed the door.

I could hear voices talking and laughing loudly below me. I wondered what could possibly be funny right now. I tried to close my eyes and sleep but I couldn't rest. After a while my sister Helene said a neighbor was here and wanted to see me. "Why couldn't she leave a message I thought." I had been through too much, what do they want from me? I got myself together and came back down the stairs. I didn't even recognize the neighbor, it was the daughter of Reverend Price, they weren't very friendly and we had never spoken. She gave me a card and a check for $50. I couldn't understand why that could not have waited.

There were more people in the house and I can't even remember who they were. I tried to go and speak to everyone, but the phone was ringing, someone was at the door, food was being brought in, someone was cooking, people were eating. It was just too much, my senses were overloaded, so I retreated back into my bedroom. Sometime during that evening my Aunt Hilda came by and asked me what I wanted for the service. I told her I couldn't think about that, that she could do it for me and it would be fine.

I spent the next few days locked in a state of confusion. I couldn't believe what was going on, and I wanted it to end. My Aunt Hilda came over again and said that we needed to pick out the clothes we wanted Courtney to wear, that her hair had been cut, and did I want to get her a wig.

I remembered that the girls had all looked so pretty in their pink dresses on Easter Sunday. I thought about that Saturday watching Courtney and Kim get their hair done at the JC Penney beauty shop, and then Courtney hiding plastic eggs with candy and money in them out in the backyard for an Easter egg hunt for Kim and Casey. I decided on the pink dress and chose some underwear.

Cornelius and I went to buy a wig at the beauty supply shop on Jefferson Street near Farmer's Market. I looked at all the wigs and hairstyles, but none of them looked like her hair or anything that a young girl would wear. I found something wrong with all of them, too long, too curly, the color wasn't right, but I had to get something. I finally found a medium length bob and bought a pair of pantyhose. I put them in the bag with the dress and underwear. Cornelius dropped me off at home first and then he took the items over to the funeral home.

The funeral director called us the next day and asked us to come and view Courtney. I was scared of the experience, scared of what I might see, and scared of what my reaction might be. I had been holding it together and I didn't want to lose it. I was numb and that's the way I wanted to stay. The house was filled with relatives but Cornelius and I wanted to go alone. It seemed like all of our movements were in slow motion within a cloudy haze. We drove in silence to the funeral home, and I thought about Courtney saying, "Mama, I'm trying to hold onto my pride and dignity," and I vowed to do the same.

When we walked through the door there were some people standing around inside the lobby. I didn't know who they were, but they were staring at us like we were walking the red carpet or something. I looked past them and followed Cornelius behind someone who led us into this room where Courtney was. We stood back for a few seconds before moving closer and I grabbed Cornelius's hand. As I approached the casket, I think I felt a little relieved. I had been afraid to see my child laying there, but this person didn't look like my Courtney, the skin color was not the same, it wasn't her face. Looking at her arm below the sleeve of the dress, it was familiar to me, I reached to touch her arm, but it was hard, it didn't feel like the skin on her arm, I didn't feel a connection to this person, it wasn't her to me. Cornelius just looked in silence. After a few minutes we left without speaking to the director.

When we exited the room my Aunt Hilda was standing there.

"What did you all think?" She asked. "I think they did a good job."

"Courtney always wore lip gloss," I told her, "I'll get some for you to give them."

We walked through the spectators in the lobby to our car and drove home.

We went through another day surrounded by a lot of family, people talking and eating, their presence was no comfort to me; there was nothing anyone could do or say to make it better. Cornelius and I talked several times about how we were both dreading the service, he said he didn't want Casey to be there, she was only two years old and didn't know what was going on and I agreed. I didn't know what to wear and I didn't feel like shopping and I needed to get my hair done. I made an appointment with Michelle at Penney's. While she did my hair I told her what had happened and she didn't know what to say. Michelle had just fixed the girls hair for Easter so she couldn't believe it. She didn't do a good job on my hair. I'm sure I blew her away with the news, but it would have to do.

The morning of the service, we dressed in silence. Cornelius and I repeating to each other that we wished we didn't have to do this. Cornelius put on his blue suit, what he called his funeral suit, because he said he had worn it to so many funerals that he couldn't wear it on any other occasion. I promised myself that I would show the courage of my big girl and hold onto my pride and dignity. I began to get nervous as we waited for the limo to pick us up and take us to the church. My stomach started the flip-turns again.

The limo came and we drove the short distance to our church. I kept Kim right under my arm as they led us down to the front of the church and I felt strange because I always preferred to sit closer to the back. We walked over to the casket to look at Courtney and Kim began to cry a little. But for me, the young girl that lay there didn't remind me of Courtney. To me, that wasn't her. I saw they had put the lip gloss on her lips. I looked at Cornelius while he looked at her and then we were lead to where we would sit.

They gave us programs and I saw Courtney's picture on the front and shuddered. Who would ever expect to see their child's picture on the front of a funeral program? I watched as other relatives went to view her, and how they cried and placed some things in there with her. Everyone came over and hugged us, giving us their condolences. I responded politely and thanked them. I was surprised that co-workers from my old job were there and they came over to speak. I smiled and thanked them for coming. Cornelius's co-workers from both of his jobs paid their respects as they shook hands and gave him hugs.

I listened to every word and every song of the service intently while I held Kim tightly. I wanted to shield her from all that was going on. I wanted her to feel protected and loved, and maybe it wouldn't be so bad. One of the soloists sang the song, "Safe in his arms" and I tried to imagine that and held onto that in my mind. Pastor Drumwright talked about the day that he had come to the hospital and prayed with us and Courtney saying "All is well."

The service was beautiful to me, and I appreciated my aunts for doing such a good job putting it together for me. It was time to go and we followed as they rolled the casket out. I kept my eyes focused straight ahead, I didn't want to make eye contact with anyone. I felt like some of them had come just wanting to see a show, like vultures who wanted to pick at my flesh.

We got into the car and while we rode I kept one arm around Kim while I looked out the window. I heard my mother and brother talking and I don't know if they were talking to Cornelius or themselves. I just kept looking out the window wondering how the rest of the world could just keep going while my world had fallen apart.

We arrived at the cemetery and walked over to the tent. A few words were said but I don't remember them. The directors asked everyone to come and place a flower down on the casket. While they came forward I just looked at the casket. It struck me that it was very pretty and I noticed her name engraved on a silver plate on the side, Courtney Nicole Brown. "I like the name too," I thought to myself remembering that night in the hospital when she said it to me, but this was not where I wanted it to be.

I remembered her name being called when she graduated from pre-school and watching her march down the aisle in a royal blue cap and gown. I was so proud my eyes had teared up and I thought about how silly I was being because this was only pre-school. What was I going to do when she graduated from high school or college, but those moments were not to be. We walked back to the car and waited to be driven to the church for the repast. As I think back we didn't touch each other and I don't know why, maybe we couldn't stand each other's pain. One of my cousins ran to the limo window to say something and all I could think about was why she hadn't come by the house to talk.

When we got to the church, Cornelius's Aunt Gladys came over to our table and asked us if we had taken any medication from a doctor. I looked at her wondering what that was about. I guess she was waiting for more fireworks. I had gone through the motions. I had kept my pride and my dignity, but I was numb. I had no understanding of what was taking place. I walked in a thick fog; voices seemed to come from a faraway place. I felt as if I existed inside of a TV screen, just watching those around me. This was like a bad movie; it could not be my life. Cornelius was withdrawn and subdued. We kept to ourselves as much as we could.

When we got home he said, "I couldn't just sit there and eat while they carried on, talking, acting like this was normal."

We were devastated, beaten down and we had to be around people who knew nothing of our struggle. Still in shock and bewildered I asked myself, "How could this happen, what went wrong, why didn't the Lord hear my prayer?"

At the house people were still coming by. I shifted into auto-pilot as my other self talked and greeted family members from my side of the family as they came by. I offered them food or something to drink, and tried to clean up as I went along. Gradually things began to calm down as relatives, friends, and neighbors went home.

One day my mother saw Courtney's glasses on the bookshelf and started telling me where I could donate them and her other things. I know she didn't mean any harm but I didn't respond because I couldn't think of anything to say that would have been respectful. I wondered if she had lost her mind. How could she think that I would want to get rid of my child's things? Why should I erase her presence from around us? Seeing her things didn't bother me, she lived here and her things should be here. What bothered me was the fact that she wasn't here.

We were going through a difficult adjustment. Kim started sleeping in the extra bed in the room with Casey. She had shared a room with Courtney all her life and guess she didn't want to be in the room alone.

The next two weeks were a blur to me. Cornelius and I rode together dropping Kim off at her summer program and Casey at the daycare. Sometimes I would have small panic attacks when I was out alone, my mind battling with memories and reality and my grief would overtake me. Cornelius spent most of his time working his frustrations off in the yard while I got groceries, cooked meals, and did a few chores around the house when I could find the energy. A few of my neighbors would call and ask if I wanted to talk, but what was there to say.

My friend and neighbor, Bonita, and I used to walk with in the evenings for exercise. One day she came by and asked if I wanted to go walking. I appreciated her caring enough to ask, but I just shook my head no. I was broken inside, I couldn't go back to doing things I used to do, nothing would ever be the same again, and there was nothing anyone could do to change that. I didn't even have the energy to walk; it took everything I had to get up in the morning.

Chapter Three

Moving On

Thoughts of Courtney filled my head and I replayed so many scenes we had while she was growing up. She was always in a rush. She walked before she was ten months old and had a maturity and depth that was far beyond her years. There was so much she wanted to do and she wanted to do it now. We were driving in the car one day and she was asking me if she could go to a teen club with her friends and I told her she would have plenty of time to go to clubs.

"Mama, you're ruining my life," she said, "What if I don't live that long?"

"Well, if you don't live that long then you've had a good life," I said back to her matter-of-factly.

I have so many mixed feelings about that conversation now that I sit without her. I second guess so many of my decisions and think maybe I should have let her do more things.

There was another occasion when I saw her sitting by herself on the loveseat in the basement and she was crying. I asked her what was wrong and she just shook her head no and said I wouldn't understand. I let it go at the time thinking it was the moodiness of a teenager. Now I wondered if she had a feeling or premonition that her life would be short.

I would spend hours laying across my bed looking at a picture on my dresser of Courtney striking a pose in her purple glittered jumpsuit from a dance performance a year ago. I wanted her back, I wanted to see her primping in the bathroom mirror. I wanted to yell for her to turn the shower water off. I wanted to hear her voice, touch her skin. I discovered that if I looked at the picture long enough her arms and legs would begin to move as if she wore dancing. I couldn't decide if my eyes were playing tricks on me or if I had found a magical photo where she came back and danced just for me.

The air of grief was thick around us, as if we existed in clear gel and every movement required intensive effort to push through the mass, to get out of bed, to shower, to eat. We weren't taking it one day at a time; it was an agonizing one minute at a time.

I became preoccupied with the John Edwards show where grieving audiences congregated in hopes of getting messages from their loved one from the other side. I could see that it only took one word of confirmation or a sign from the person they lost to uplift their hearts and relieve their sorrows. I secretly wished I could get in that audience and have him bring Courtney from the other side. I needed that confirmation that he gave some of those in the audience, her sign telling me that she was okay.

The saddest families in the audience were the ones who had lost children. I guess that it's true that misery loves company because it comforted me to see I wasn't alone in my grief, that I wasn't the only one hurting. John Edwards talked about looking for signs that your loved one is giving you and I prayed and hoped everyday for some sign. I searched for Courtney in my dreams, but they were only filled with darkness, she wouldn't come to me.

It's hard losing a child because you feel that maybe they are lost or alone in this other place. I believe in promises of God, I believe in heaven, but she's my baby. You need to be there with them, you want to go with them. It's like watching a kid go to school all alone. You just want to walk with them and make sure they get to the right place. I prayed that my Dad was there, that he had met her and he was taking care of her, that my Grandmother and my Aunt Cassandra would not let me down and would comfort her. Whenever I was alone I would talk to Courtney, tell her I loved her and missed her and ask her to show me a sign that she was okay.

At the end of the third week, Cornelius said it was time for us to go back to work. I didn't think I was ready and I wanted to tell him I needed more time, but I didn't want to add to his stress by being difficult. If he was going to try to get back to our lives and move forward, I was going to try also.

When I dropped Casey off at the daycare I felt all the eyes watching me, some out of pity, and some with curiosity as I took Casey to her classroom. When I arrived with Kim at her Fisk mini-college program there were more looks of sympathy and some even avoided looking. Then I made the dreaded drive to Vanderbilt. It felt terrible coming back there. It was like returning to the scene of the crime. I boarded the shuttle at the parking lot fighting the urge to turn around and go back home to the security of my closed doors.

My boss at the time was one of the most gracious people that I have ever met. His name was Roberto Cruz-Gervis and he was from Guatemala. Roberto was a medical doctor finishing up a research collaboration in the Pulmonary Department. He was very tall and handsome with a lot of style. I loved how put together he was every day. His hair was always neatly cut and styled, and his clothes were always immaculate and tastefully coordinated down to his socks.

Roberto was the director of the Intensive Care Unit at Meharry and he had a research fellowship to study cystic fibrosis. I was his lab manager and the person who did his research experiments. He had been kind and very supportive through the whole ordeal, and had come to visit with Courtney in the hospital before her surgery. Roberto even came to the funeral service and made it a point to tell me he was so sorry for my loss. The day I came back to work he knew that it was difficult for me to be there. He told me to just do what I could, to take care of myself, and that he would try to get through the process of paperwork for getting his lab space ready on the Meharry Campus so I wouldn't have to come to the Vanderbilt Campus to work.

I knew that I blamed the Vanderbilt staff for what I considered to be a lack of treatment and professionalism during our clinic visits and the consideration and thorough examination that I felt Courtney didn't receive. Whenever I thought about how much pain and suffering my child had gone through as we kept coming back and forth to the clinic it made me very angry. I also didn't like the fact that we weren't really told how serious her condition was after she was admitted. We might not have let them operate. We may have opted to take her to the St. Jude's Children's Hospital in Memphis. Now it was too late to change the past mistakes, there was nothing that could be done.

I walked through the hallway on the first floor of Medical Center North and it was if I had never been there before, although I had worked in that building for more than ten years. A few people stopped me as I walked to give me their condolences. I felt raw, like I was wearing my skin on the inside out, and I seemed to burn all over. I rubbed my hand over my forearm and could feel the pain from my own touch. I didn't get anything accomplished that morning. Somehow I made it to lunch time and went home. I watched another episode of John Edwards talking to people on the other side before I had to pick up the kids.

I went through this routine for several days. One afternoon as I sat on the couch a feeling of uneasiness grew and began to turn into panic inside of me, like I was in danger and it scared me. I felt like something bad was going to happen but I didn't know what. I could feel it getting closer and I felt like I needed to run. I stood up to rush for the phone to call Cornelius but before I could get to the phone it was if I was hit over the back of the head by something or someone. I fell to the floor halfway to the phone and began to scream and scream at the top of my lungs. I could hear myself screaming Courtney's name. I had that feeling of being two people again. I knew a part of me was hysterical and it was scaring me, but at the same time I couldn't control it. I don't know how long I lay on the floor screaming, except somehow by 4:00 I had screamed and cried myself out and pulled it together enough to pick up the kids. I tried to put ice and cold water on my swollen face and red eyes. I didn't want Kim to be upset knowing I had been crying. It helped the redness some but not much and I was totally congested.

    The last bit of numbness or shock was gone and I had to face the reality, I wasn't in a bad dream. Driving home from the daycare with the girls in the car I was in such unbearable pain, not just emotional or mental, but I was in physical pain. I ached all over and my chest throbbed and I felt like I couldn't stand it much longer. As I drove I looked at the cars in the opposite lane and I thought about driving into the oncoming traffic where I could just end it. If I simply crossed over into the other lane it would all be over. The pain would end. I would find Courtney and we would all be together again.

    My thoughts were racing so fast I couldn't keep up and then I heard the girls playing in the back seat and the music on the radio and it brought me back to my senses.

    "What is wrong with me?" I said quietly.

    These girls had suffered with us and they deserved a chance to live and a chance to be happy. I knew Courtney would want them to have a chance to grow up and fulfill their dreams. She had always been so protective of them, hurting them would only hurt her more, and I couldn't do that. I remembered Cornelius's words from the hospital saying that we weren't going to let this devastate us. How could I take this tragedy and pain and multiply it. I decided in the car that afternoon that I would dedicate my life to my girls. I would do everything I could to protect them, to keep them healthy and happy, and to help their dreams come true. They deserved to live, and they were my only reason for living.

***

One morning I was struggling with every step I took. My Aunt Lillie, who ran the daycare at the church, saw me from her office window and came out.

"How are you, Karen?" she asked.

"I am so tired," I told her.

"Come on in here, I have something for you," she said.

She handed me a book of prayers called *The Weapons of Our Warfare*, and she turned to a prayer that said, "When you need Physical Strength to Keep Going." I took it and pasted a smile on my face before I left.

When I got to work I read the prayer. Then I turned the pages through the rest of the book. It was filled with prayers for most every situations that arises in our lives. There were other prayers that I read that gave me the comfort and strength I needed to get through the day. They were like meditations, especially the prayer for when you have been hurt or disappointed. There was a prayer for peace based on the 23rd Psalm, a prayer for your young children, a prayer for your husband, and one for praise and thanksgiving. That prayer book became my lifeline and I never left home without it.

It wasn't long before Roberto had gotten the clearance to move his research over to his lab space at Meharry and that helped a lot. It meant that I didn't have to go to Vanderbilt and deal with the emotional baggage I had there, and not being able to breathe until I got off the campus. On my first day at Meharry, I got out my prayer book and read the daily prayer, then I read the prayer of praise and thanksgiving, then I prayed for my children and then Cornelius, and then for peace. I would sing out loud to myself. There were the verses of some hymns I had collected in church that I was keeping in my prayer book, It Is Well with My Soul, My Faith Looks Up to Thee, and We'll Understand It Better By and By. It became a ritual that I went through every morning. Sometimes it took close to an hour, but it was what got me through the day.

The minutes turned to hours and then into days and weeks, but they were still very hard. There were so many firsts to go through. There was the first time of going to church without her, sitting there on the pew in agony. I felt like I was on fire. The first Father's Day, I bought a card and signed her name, I couldn't bear Cornelius not getting a card from her and I could see he appreciated it. Even the first 4th of July was hard. Courtney loved fireworks and we would buy a bunch and shoot them off in front of the house after it got dark. We all went to her memorial and shot off three rockets and for a moment I felt like we were connected again.

The grief came in tsunami waves. At times it seemed like the open wound had finally crusted over, and then it would hit again. Once I cried all the way home, barely able to see to drive. When I got home I stood in the garage and screamed at the top of my lungs. Cornelius hadn't left for work yet. I knew he could hear me, but he didn't come down. I didn't fault him for his inability to deal with my pain; I knew he was going through a hell of his own. Courtney was a Daddy's girl since birth and they were very close.

When he first started working a second job at Davidson Transit, she was around three years old. She cried herself to sleep for two weeks, yelling "I want my daddy" until she passed out. It was at some of the rough times in our marriage when I thought about leaving, I would look at them and know I could never separate them.

Your mind is always filled with so many questions and what-ifs, what if it the tumor was caused by something in our environment, is it in our genes, could the other girls have the same thing? Could she have survived if we had discovered it sooner? How would I have explained to her that the doctors hadn't got the entire tumor? Would the suffering from the chemotherapy been too miserable for her to bear? Would she have deteriorated more and did I have the courage to watch her suffer? Would any extra time we could have had been of any quality? I started to thank God for His infinite wisdom that if we couldn't keep her that she did not have to suffer needlessly. I've always heard that the Lord wouldn't put more on you than you could bear, I had my doubts, but maybe he had been merciful to us after all.

One day the Woodlawn Cemetery office called and said that they had placed the marker down. It was during the week and Cornelius was working both jobs that day and I needed to see it. I remembered how emotional I felt when I saw my Aunt Cassandra's headstone for the first time and how shocking it was to see her name there. It took my breath away and it made everything real and final. From that experience, I didn't know how I would react to see Courtney's. I went over to the houses of my three Aunts who lived near the cemetery to see if they were home and if one of them would go with me. I surely didn't want to go alone, but no one was home.

I decided I had to see it and I couldn't wait. I drove nervously over to the cemetery and made the left turn onto the grounds. I started looking for the large tree that was there in the Garden of Ruth section, knowing the spot where the marker would be nearby. I parked when I saw the tree. I got out of the car and walked slowly over to the area. Then I saw it, *Courtney Nicole Brown, beloved daughter and sister, always in our hearts*. As many times as the reality hits you, it is still unfathomable. I felt too weak to stand and sat down in the grass.

"Why O Lord?" I pleaded. "Why did you take my baby? She deserved to live, she was a good girl."

After a while of drowning in my sorrow, I thanked the Lord for her life, for blessing me to have her for those fourteen years. I talked to her for a while, prayed for a while, and then as I quieted down I looked around the grounds. I began to see myself sitting there all alone, in a cemetery, at the foot of my daughter's memorial. It was a sad sight, even to me.

Chapter Four
Getting Stronger

I would go into the Courtney's bedroom often to look at her things. I would go into the closet and smell her clothes for her scent. Sometimes I would lay in the spot between the bed and the wall and try to feel her presence there. I wanted to see what she saw from that spot and how it felt to her. On one particular day as I was on my way out of the room I saw Kim's journal on her bed. I stopped to pick it up and began to read it. I wasn't prepared for what I read. We all held our emotions together so well when we were around each other. Yet on this paper she described standing in front of the knife block in the kitchen and wanting to take one of them out and kill herself, she missed Courtney so bad, and didn't want to live.

I was horrified. I couldn't lose another child. After I picked them up from daycare and the summer program, I called Kim into the kitchen and I started talking to her about how we had to stick together and how much I needed her. I wanted to keep it light.

"We've been through some hard things together," I said. "I'm here for you girl and I need you to be here for me."

She just looked at me with her big brown eyes opened wide. I tried to joke with her and grabbed her hand and started singing the song by Destiny's Child, "I'm a Survivor." I changed the words to "we are survivors, we're not going to give up, we're gonna work harder, cause we're surviving." She started to laugh because I was getting some of the words wrong, but I just kept singing and dancing and I told her to join in and she finally did. We just sang, "I'm a survivor, cause I'm surviving" with my wrong wording and acted so silly. It became our battle cry and whenever I thought she was having a moment or feeling down we would just start singing it wrong words and all until we started laughing.

When the summer was coming to a close I thought it was probably time to take Casey out of her baby bed and move her into Courtney and Kim's room. I changed the room around a bit and changed the direction of Courtney's bed to open the space in the room a bit more even though a part of me wanted to leave everything as it was. Casey did very well and loved having a big girl bed. I still wasn't able to move Courtney's clothes out of her closet; everything was still as she had left them. Casey was in a new bedroom but her clothes and toys stayed in the other room. She was young and didn't know any different. When the summer ended and school started back things were becoming more settled and routine.

Then one evening I got a phone call from Metro Schools.

"We're calling you to see why Courtney hasn't been to school," the caller said.

I had to say the words that I had not ever said before, "Courtney passed away."

"I'm so sorry," the woman on the other end said sincerely. "I apologize for the call and I will correct the records."

I was blown away, it was hard to say those words, and even today those are words that I can't say. Holidays were rough because Courtney loved every one of them, Halloween, Thanksgiving, and especially Christmas. Cornelius always spoiled the girls, buying them most if not all of what they wanted. Shopping was difficult, I saw so many things that I would have liked to give her, things I knew she would want. I even bought gifts for everybody from her, and somehow we got through. I remember days when I would stand in the Hallmark card aisle at Walgreens to buy a card for some occasion and I would drift down to the sympathy cards and read them, particularly those for parents who had lost a child, the words were so comforting and I would read one after another as if they had been sent especially for me.

    Courtney was born on St. Patrick's Day and she celebrated it like she was Irish. The day before I had gone to Walgreens and bought her a birthday card and I wrote her a letter. On her birthday we did all the things that she liked to do to celebrate her birthday. We drove to Kentucky to play the lotto, Courtney always thought we would win one day so for her we bought tickets. We bought some birthday balloons and a green pinwheel. Next we went to the cemetery to change her flowers and tied one of the balloons onto the vase. We read the 23rd Psalm, her favorite scripture, and sang happy birthday Stevie Wonder style. Driving out of Woodlawn we all watched the balloon floating and the pinwheel spinning in the breeze.

    Courtney also loved to eat at O'Charley's on her birthday and get the waiters and waitresses to sing the birthday song at the table. I ordered the fried chicken salad which was her favorite food on the menu to eat there. When we got home we gave Kim and Casey each a balloon and went out on the deck. We sang Happy Birthday, let them go, and watched them float up higher and higher until they disappeared. I kept one to leave in the house.

    A few weeks later I was sitting watching an old movie when out of the side of my eye I saw the deflated balloon float into the doorway of the bonus room. I was transfixed as I watch it slowly keep moving further into the room. I wondered if air from somewhere or something was blowing it. "What's moving it?" I thought. Maybe there's a draft. I kept watching and the balloon floated low on the floor over to me and then rose up into my lap. That's when I knew that she was there and she was giving me the sign that I had begged for. I was deeply touched and all I could do was cry. I told her I loved her and thanked her for being my daughter.

"I knew you would come to me," I said out loud.

It just lifted my spirits so much, but I wanted more, I needed her home with me. I used to imagine driving around in town and seeing her walking down the street and then I would pull over to her saying, "Courtney, we have been looking for you. Get in this car girl so we can go home." But it was just a fantasy along with the others, that I would wake up from this nightmare and this awful thing had never happened.

I dressed the girls in baby blue for Easter and they looked so pretty. I was about to take their picture and I just couldn't take a picture without Courtney being in it. It felt like we were going on without her and that's something I didn't want to do. I gave Kim a photo of Courtney to hold in her lap to help me. I wondered if I making them crazy with all my weirdness.

As the anniversary came closer I knew I didn't want to be there, in our house or even in the city. I didn't want any phone calls, I didn't want to talk about it. I started making plans to take a trip out of town. Cornelius and I decided to go to Chattanooga. It was a short drive and there were things in the city that the kids would enjoy seeing. From the start the getting away didn't help much, it was hard to take a trip without her in that spot over my right shoulder. Kim had started sitting in her seat at the dinner table and in the car, but it wasn't the same. During the trip Cornelius was very moody. We took the girls to Look Out Mountain and rode the tram, but his heart wasn't in it. We tried to have a good time but the sadness was too heavy to carry and we came home a day early.

***

Through all of the hurt Casey was such a blessing to all of us. She was too young to understand what had happened and she was the only one of us not weighed down by grief. She would make us laugh with her antics and as a toddler she kept us busy. I thought back to when I found out I was pregnant with her and how I was so upset. Kim was seven years old at the time and Courtney was eleven. Cornelius was working two jobs all the time and I didn't have much help with the girls. The thought of starting over with a new baby depressed me. I had complained so much, sometimes I wonder if I was punished for it.

After Courtney got sick, I hurt so bad. I wondered if I would have felt this badly if something would have happened to my other girls. I wondered if it would have hurt less if it was Casey because she was just a baby. I wondered if I was partial to Courtney because she was my first born. I got my answers soon enough.

Kim had a sore throat and I took her to get her throat checked out. We went to a new pediatrician needless to say, and she prescribed an antibiotic. I filled the prescription and dropped Kim off at home. I gave her one of the pills before I left and went back to finish a few things at work. I hadn't been there very long before I got a phone call from Kim. She was telling me that she couldn't breathe. I panicked. What if it was an allergic reaction to the penicillin? I just got up and flew out the door with my keys. I couldn't go through this again.

While I was driving I realized that I should have called 911 before I left the lab but I didn't think I had time to go back. I got to my car and just started driving like a bat out of hell. I beeped my horn and just went around the other cars even when the light was red. I knew I was driving reckless and I began to worry that if I had an accident I would never get there, but I couldn't stop, I had to hurry. I pressed down on the gas and speeded up Clarksville Highway beeping my horn like I was an emergency vehicle. I almost wanted the police to come after me so I could get their help. When I got to the house I didn't pull into the garage. I stopped and ran right up to the front door. Then I realized I didn't have my door keys. I rang the door bell and Kim answered it. She was fine. The allergic reaction was minimal; she had just felt some tightness in her throat. I gave her a Benadryl tablet. After that, all I could do was plop down on the steps inside the door. I was drained completely. That experience woke me up. I needed to appreciate what I did have instead of worrying so much about what I had lost.

    I got another lesson just in case the point needed to be reinforced. I took the girls to work with me one Saturday afternoon. I had an experiment running that I need to collect samples for over the weekend, but it would take less than an hour. It was something I did from time to time with the plan we would do something fun together when I was finished. I got the kids situated in the lab where they could occupy themselves with the computer on the desk and got to work. Periodically I would come back to the office to check on them.

    I had a candy jar that set on the desk with large individual wrapped lifesavers and they loved to raid it whenever they came. I had some time between tasks so I went to watch them for a minute to make sure they didn't get too carried away on the computer. Suddenly Casey took a breath to say something, I don't know what, but the lifesaver got stuck in her throat. She looked straight at me and I knew she couldn't breathe. I was instantly horrified. I dropped whatever I had in my hands rushed over and grabbed her out of the chair and started doing the Heimlich maneuver on her. I yelled to Kim to call the police and as I rushed up the hallway to the elevator with Casey draped over my arms while I continued to do the Heimlich rushing down the hallway. I heard Kim's horrified voice screaming behind me that she didn't know the number or where we were but I didn't have the time to go back and help her. Just as I was about to turn the corner, Casey gagged, and the purple lifesaver hit the floor. I stopped where we were and let her feet drop to the ground. I could breathe again, the madness was over. I was so relieved but I was a nervous wreck shaking from the inside out.

    "Thank you Lord," I whispered.

    When we got back to the lab, Kim was crying nearly

hysterically. I got her calmed down and I told her not to worry that Casey was okay and that I should have given her the number for emergency and that she did fine. I salvaged the experiment and we went straight home.

I told Cornelius at the door, "I can't take anymore," and I climbed the steps to go to bed.

I didn't even have the energy to tell him what happened until later on in the evening. I had learned my lesson. I love all my girls the same, they all mean the world to me, and the loss of either would have been the same grief and hurt. I prayed for the health and safety of my girls, and that the number of their days would be fulfilled.

***

During that winter, near the holidays, a bush that grew in our front yard that usually bloomed once in the spring, bloomed in the winter's freezing temperatures. The tree had no leaves, just the white balls of flowers that stood out against the brown grass of the season. I knew it was a sign, a gift from Courtney. I would stand at the window and just look out at the bush knowing it was my miracle. It sent me off each morning and greeted me when I came home. When it rained and the ice froze on the blossoms they didn't wilt and sustained me through the winter.

My neighbor, Mr. Wright, walked by one day while I was looking at it.

"What kind of tree is that blooming in the winter?"

"I don't know," I told him with a smile.

It didn't matter to me what kind of tree it was. It was my miracle tree and it encouraged me that life does go on under the harshest conditions.

As time went on we got stronger and the kids got older and things began to get a little easier. We took some more trips together and slowly I think we began to laugh again, not just on the outside, but on the inside too. I remember the big snowstorm of Nashville in February of 2003. The snow starting to fall around 10:00 in the morning and the news was projecting ten inches before nightfall. The college president sent an e-mail advising all non-essential personnel that the college was closing and to take care on their travel home. School closing had already been announced. When I left the building the snow was coming like white blankets thrown over the streets and sidewalks. Walking to my car I knew it was too late, it was already too deep and I couldn't make it. I went back to the Basic Science building and called Cornelius. He said he was leaving work and would stop and pick me up and then we would pick up the girls. NES was less than ten minutes away but it took him an hour to get to Meharry.

When he finally got there he was driving his small blue 1989 Nissan truck. I climbed in and then we headed to John Early to pick up Kim. The whole city was shutting down and cars were stranded on every corner and some in the middle of the road. It was more snow that I had seen anywhere in over twenty years. It was as beautiful as it was an inconvenience. Once we made the three turns to pick up Casey from Hull Jackson we could finally head home. The steep rise on Clarksville Highway was taking out every car that dared to make the attempt to pass.

Cornelius parked at the church at the bottom of the hill and said that we would have to walk the rest of the way. He carried Casey on his shoulders and Kim and I trudged along beside them. The big flakes were still falling heavily and I felt like we were the characters that you see within a decorative snow globe. That struggle up the hill in the snow somehow bonded us together. We were cold and it had been a long afternoon but I felt invigorated. Making it through that storm together felt good, like we could make it through anything. We were still a family.
***

When the spring arrived I must have had spring fever. I felt like I wanted to breakout and grow like the trees and flowers.

I wanted to get out the monotony of my life and do something different. I made a commitment to try to visit someplace I had never been before each year. That year I decided that I wanted to take the kids to Disney World, besides I had never been to Florida. It was something I had always looked forward to doing with Courtney and Kim before Casey was born. I had been waiting for when they got older where they could remember and treasure the experience and then Casey came along.

    I regretted the fact that I would never get to take Courtney to places and do things that I had postponed. I vowed never to put off doing things at the right moment and to make as many good memories together as we could whenever we could. Disney World was exhausting but great and the girls loved it, except all the while I felt we weren't complete. Family time is often taken for granted, but I can't think of anything more important. I'm so thankful for the precious memories and time that we did have. I imagined that Courtney was there with us and was somehow enjoying all of the fun.

Chapter Five

Growing Pains

We made it through the next year with the normal challenges that go with raising a family. I took care of the kids, worked, and watched a lot of TV while Cornelius purged all of his frustrations working in the yard. We had established a routine and basically lived our lives on auto-pilot.

My work day usually consisted of one hour of prayer and meditation, then I did my experiments, and guided a graduate student that had joined the lab a couple of years back. The lab was very productive and Roberto was satisfied with the amount of data that we were able to produce. He was a boss who focused on results and not on hours. His policy was that once you were finished with what you could accomplish for that day, you didn't have to hang around killing time. It motivated you to get as much done as you could in fewer hours. So because I didn't take a lunch break most days I was done between 1:00 and 2:00. This worked perfectly for me.

I found that if I didn't tire myself out and didn't allow myself to get stressed, I could control my emotions better. It's similar to being handicapped and finding ways to deal with your limitations. So I worked hard at taking care of myself and getting plenty of rest. I learned that if I didn't feel like cooking or cleaning, don't do it, it's not the end of the world. The important thing was to maintain my sense of well-being or rather my sanity to take care of Kim and Casey and hold our family together.

I began to notice Kim being harsh and mean at times with

Casey when they interacted together. It bothered me because Courtney had been so gentle and kind to her as a big sister. I wanted them to have a good relationship because they only had each other. I knew from my own experience that unresolved issues between siblings carry on into adulthood and can ruin family relationships for a lifetime. I had an idea of what it was, because I had fought the same reaction myself. I sat down with her to discuss it.

Kim told me that Casey gets on her nerves and messes with her things and it makes her angry. I explained that Casey is just a little girl and she's not trying to do anything to upset her. I told her that I knew that there were moments when she was mad at Casey because she wasn't Courtney and that it was a natural reaction. I said that it was something that we have to control because if it wasn't for Casey we would have had a harder time, that the Lord had known what the plan was and blessed us with Casey to cushion our pain.

***

One afternoon I was looking at pictures from a few years back in the study and reflecting on memories before our lives had changed so drastically when I noticed a small plastic bag with a hospital sticker on the outside on one of the shelves. I opened it up and it had Courtney's hair in it. I didn't know if it was the hair from the procedure they did in her hospital room or if it was the hair they shaved from her head before surgery. It was in long wavy locks from when I had braided her hair while she was in the hospital. I could see the different textures from the curly new growth of hair and the permed hair. Holding this hair in my hand was like touching Courtney again, feeling her again. I brought the handful of hair to my nose and smelled it and it had her scent as fresh as the day when I last combed her hair. I looked at the hair knowing it was the most precious thing I had in the entire house. I carefully placed it back in the plastic bag and tied it back carefully to preserve the scent of her on it and placed it back on the shelf. On days when I missed her most I would take down the bag and touch her hair and feel a part of her in my hand again and it comforted me.

***

Four years had gone by, but it seemed like in some ways time had stood still. One afternoon in August of 2004, Roberto came over to the lab to talk, most of the time he was so busy. I usually didn't see him for months at a time so I knew it was important. He mentioned that his wife had recently gotten accepted to Harvard and was ready to go back to school. He explained how she had waited for him to finish his internship and get his medical career established.

Roberto talked about how she had followed him wherever he needed to go and he wanted to return to her this same opportunity to follow her dream. He said that they had found a house in Boston and they would be moving in a few weeks. Roberto said he was sorry for the inconvenience to me and explained that my position would last for about two more months at Meharry, enough time to allow me to complete the project we had been collaborating on with a lab at Emory University. I told him that I understood his decision although I was devastated in a way. But I couldn't help but be happy for him and his family, he had been so good to me and good for me. Roberto was a monumental blessing for me, he cared when I needed it and had given me space and time to heal.

The more Roberto talked about their plans the more my anxiety level rose. What would I do, where would I work? This was my comfort zone. Could I make it in another lab and work a full day? I had been in several other labs and I wondered if I could survive in that stressful environment again, working around larger groups of people and dealing with their different personalities while being pushed to the limit. The bottom line was that I knew that I had to work. Cornelius and I were still wrestling with daily living expenses, and the financial strain of our old house that we struggled to keep rented made things even tighter. I realized that the inner trooper was about to be called back on duty.

I used to be teased about being a trooper when Courtney was born. I had passed my due date and one of the doctors in the group I used for prenatal care suggested I come into the hospital to induce labor. I hadn't been there an hour before they gave me the Pitocin and the contractions started immediately. Cornelius and I had taken some Lamaze classes and I started doing the breathing exercise we learned in the birthing classes. After about eight hours of huffing and puffing and getting to five centimeters, they finally gave me an epidural which eased the contractions some, but the labor continued for another 12 hours.

No matter how hard it got I refused to lose my cool. I was always a reserved type who never liked to make a scene, but I was getting tired.

"Cornelius, I can't take it anymore," I said, "I'm getting ready to start screaming."

He got a little nervous and he said, "No, Karen, just hold on, keep doing what you're doing."

A few minutes later an intern came in and told us that the baby was showing signs of distress and they were going to do a C-section.

"You sure have been a trooper," he said.

Throughout that whole experience I think I had been called a trooper about four times by four different people. So whenever situations got tough or I got tired Cornelius would say, "You know you're a trooper."

So here I go again, time to update my resume and get out there and find myself another job. Roberto had given me a glowing recommendation letter, but there were only so many places you could work in Nashville in research besides

Vanderbilt. Over the next few weeks I had one interview at the Dupont research lab in Clarksville, TN for working on paint and resins for cars. They had a nice group of white guys there who were looking for someone they could not only work well with, but someone who would fit into their social circle. One look at me and I knew they were having their doubts. When I didn't hear back from them I wasn't surprised and that was fine, the commute was 45 minutes each way, a little long for me to pick up the kids on time and Cornelius was unable to help with his work schedule.

I had received a few calls from research labs at Vanderbilt, my last resort, and as my paid time began to shorten I had no choice but to consider them. Looking at the Vanderbilt job website there weren't many positions for lab managers, but I didn't want our financial situation to get desperate so I applied for both research assistant II and III positions even though that was taking two steps back in classification and pay.

I scheduled an interview with Dr. Naresh Patel in the Microbiology Department for a research assistant II position. He was taller with a heavier build than most of the Indian men I had met, and he also had a limp. He had the look of a man of academia, carrying himself with that air of superiority as he showed me around his lab. He told me that he had patented an insecticide that was sold on the commercial market for which he received a good bit of money. I must say I was impressed with his accomplishments, but I just needed a job.

He mentioned the extent of my experience and abilities in the laboratory from the recommendations that I had given him, and that he really needed someone who could work independently because he also ran another lab at a University in Texas and was out of town quite often. I told him that I had no problem with that and I worked well independently. Dr. Patel invited me to have lunch with him and his lab technician and it was quite comfortable. We talked casually about our children, how many we all had, their ages, and what they like to do as we walked to the Panera Bread restaurant two blocks down on 21st Ave. When we returned to the lab he offered me the job. It was a pay cut of over $7 thousand, but it definitely beat a blank. I was to start the following week. He would be out of town, but he would leave some reading material and a copy of his grant for me to get familiar with the work of the lab.

    I tried to prepare myself for this new job, knowing I would have to work the full eight hours, pick up the kids and then take them to their afternoon activities. They were both taking tap and ballet classes at the Centennial Arts and Activity Center, but Kim was also swimming and playing basketball for Rose Park Middle school. I always believed in keeping my girls busy, it burned off a lot of moodiness and frustration that growing kids have, but it ran me ragged.

    Naresh was out of town as he said when I came in for my first day, so I got acquainted with Marla, his lab technician. Marla was between forty and fort-five, slim and fit, and kind of reminded me of a hippie or a very earthy person. She had managed a restaurant with her husband before their divorce. She mentioned that she had been working for Dr. Patel for a few years, they had met through mutual friends. Marla said that she had never been in science and had learned her lab skills on the job. We laughed about it and I told her that most of the people in science and research had started off to do something else before they landed in a research lab and then spent the rest of their careers trying to branch into something else that paid better.

    Naresh was away for about two weeks, and I occupied myself with reading his grant and learning what kinds of things Marla did in the lab. I helped her with her work and some small experiments that he had requested to be done while he was out of town. The morning when he returned he called me in his office to talk. I went in and sat down.

    "So what have you come up with?" he asked.

"I read the grant and the papers that you gave me," I responded.

Then he said, "Karen, I gave you that reading material for you to design a research project for studying malaria."

"I didn't realize that you wanted me to design a project based on that," I said.

"I hired you because you said that you could work independently, and you are making excuses for not having a plan," he said indignantly.

Now I know I have been doing lab research for nearly 15 years, but I only have a B.S. in Chemistry. I have worked with principal investigators assisting them with their research. The research assistants are basically the P.I.'s hands, but I was determined not to get started on the wrong foot.

"What are the steps to studying malaria," I asked him.

He looked at me like I was wasting his time and said, "You can find out by going to the library and doing a search on the subject."

"Alright, I can do that," I said, standing up to leave his office.

So I spent the next few days in the library pulling papers related to Malaria. In any medical research you first have to ask an intelligent question about an approach to the solution based on your scientific knowledge. First, I didn't have a strong enough scientific background to ask a question based on what was already known and where I wanted to go. Secondly, after you determine the question you need to answer you need to determine the experiments that will assist you in answering the question.

I kept asking myself, what did this man want for $31 thousand? Was I supposed to, by some form of magic, pull the cure for Malaria out of my head or out of the library? If he could give me a base or some idea of what he had in mind or where he would like to start that would have been helpful. It turned out that he didn't know anything about malaria, that it was an area he was thinking about branching out into. He should have hired a post-doctoral candidate who had previously studied malaria, but he wanted a bargain.

I spent the next month walking all over campus trying to see what method he would use for the study, who was working on something similar, and who had some samples we could use. Naresh went out of town again for about ten days, when he returned and I didn't have any data for him to see, he said that things weren't going to work out because I wasn't able to work independently. It bothered me because he was being totally unrealistic, but that was a losing battle. He had hired a research assistant II and wanted them to set up a malaria study and run it for him while he ran his other lab in Texas. That was his right, except I couldn't do it, and for the money he was paying me I didn't even want to try.

    I must admit that I was somewhat relieved to get out of that lab because my skin was starting to itch again and that's when I know I'm getting stressed out. I knew that to function well and dodge the land mines of sadness and depression I couldn't go there. So I was back where I started, having to look for a job.

Chapter Six

Out Of My Comfort Zone

It was about a month later in March of 2005 that I got another call for an interview at Vanderbilt. It was with a new researcher in the Cell Biology Department. I had worked in the department over ten years back, but I had a great relationship with my past boss and he had recommended me highly. So there I was again back at Vanderbilt, definitely not where I wanted to be, but I had to stay focused on what's best for my family. I met with her in her lab area located in the Medical Research Building III. It was the brand new research laboratory facility on campus.

Her name was Irina Ivanov, and she was Russian. Petite and soft spoken, her hair was dyed a bright red that accentuated the paleness of her skin and her ice blue eyes. She told me she needed someone who could catch on quickly because large amounts of money had been invested in buying her this super microscope and she was under a lot of pressure to produce data. There was nothing new there, all researchers are under tremendous pressure to produce and publish.

She made me an offer that was similar to the one I had just come out of, a position as a research assistant II with a salary of about $32 thousand. I told her that I would be happy to work with her project, that I liked to learn new things, and that her project sounded interesting. What I really thought was that people sure had high expectations tied to low salaries. I started working for her the next week.

That first morning, we talked about the things she would need to set up her lab, from large equipment down to paper towels. I had set up research labs twice before, so I went about ordering the necessary supplies. Irina was different as most people are from different cultures. She would sometimes come out of her office into the lab and turn back around as if she had forgotten something and then never come back. It struck me kind of funny but sometimes people in academia, and I should say in the entire world, have strange habits.

Setting up a lab involves a lot of things that don't necessarily come under your job description, like putting together tables and shelves, taking the doors off of refrigerators and changing the hinges to open on the opposite side, and running her errands to Target. I usually go with the flow and do some of the things that maintenance would do as a show of goodwill particularly if I am the only employee.

Once we got the supplies in and the solutions made, she began to train me on the hundreds of thousand dollar microscope. The microscope was amazing and I couldn't believe we could actually see this much within one cell. I had done tissue culture and grown cells in petri dishes before, but we were plating cells on a glass just a bit larger than a contact lens. It was very tedious. You had to be careful to hold the glass firmly, but not so firm that you crack it or break it. I was doing pretty well with them, until one morning, I didn't grip the slide firmly enough in my attempt not to crack it and it slipped from the tweezers. Irina had a fit, scolding me about how she told me I had to be careful and that I had ruined the experiment, although it was just one plate out of sixteen. I apologized to calm things down, and she insisted that she would do it herself and for me to watch. As fate would have it, she dropped a slide, we both stayed silent, what more needed to be said.

Experiments in research sometimes have incubation times or running times that may last up to two hours or longer. One day during an incubation I was reading some news articles on the computer.

Irina came over and said, "I'm not comfortable with you using the computer unless it's for ordering supplies."

"Okay," I told her, "Not a problem."

The next day I brought a book from home to occupy the time when I was waiting during run times.

It wasn't long before Irina said, "I would rather you not read books while you are at work."

"Okay, that's fine," I responded, shutting the book.

I talked to some co-workers I knew in other labs because it was a little unusual. They laughed and thought it was weird but it was nothing you can do about it. Most labs had more than one person and passed time talking with one another.

Cornelius recommended that I just get out of the lab more, so she wouldn't be irritated. So whenever I had a long incubation I would walk across campus and back to get some exercise. About six weeks after I had been working with Irina, she called me into her office.

"I'm not happy," she said. "You're not working as hard as you can, and you're doing things you're not supposed to."

I responded saying, "You said you don't want me to use the computer, so I don't, you said you didn't want me to read, so I don't. I'm doing all the things in the lab, I can't rush them any faster, what do you want me to do?"

"When you have time between experiments you can get a wash cloth and wipe down the cabinets and the walls in the lab," she said in a matter-of-fact manner.

Well it was official, she was slightly crazy. I was not the cleaning woman. I didn't go to college so I could do housekeeping's job. The conversation caught me off guard and I didn't know how to respond so I did my best to keep my face expressionless. I felt like she had insulted me, but she was my boss and I didn't want to overstep my bounds. After a few moments I stood up and left her office.

It wasn't bad enough that I was underpaid and unappreciated, but I was not going to be the maid. She was one of those bosses who think they have purchased you for eight hours and they want some work out of you for every minute. I realized that all the times that I thought she had forgotten something when she came out of her office and then turned back around, she was really spying on me.

As time went on the work environment was really bothering me. I didn't feel like I was being respected as an employee. I went to the department administrator, Jim Hensen, to discuss how to handle it. Jim told me that Irina had already been there to talk to him and was upset too. He advised me to just do what I could to make her happy as long as it was within reason. He also mentioned that with the new policies after 9-11 everyone had to submit copies of their degree and they needed a copy of mine. I told him thanks and I would request a copy.

This made my heart beat faster as panic began to build; Tennessee State had never mailed me a copy of my diploma and I had never asked why. Honestly at the time I didn't want to know why. There were only two reasons why they wouldn't send it. I either owed money or there was some deficiency in the requirements for my degree. That was seventeen years ago and I knew there was going to be some drama. I called the records office and they referred me to the undergraduate school. I called the office and set an appointment with Dr. Jones, the dean of the undergraduate school who would check on the matter for me.

Meanwhile things were getting worse at work. I ignored Irina's suggestion that I should be the clean-up woman whenever I had free minutes at work and this ruined our working relationship. She may have perceived it as being defiant or insubordinate, but I considered it insulting to a professional. Irina was stomping around and giving me the mad face most of the time. She would walk by all through the day to see what I was doing. I began to feel like I was in a cage or a prisoner at work.

I was starting to itch again and I knew that was a sign that

I was getting stressed. My arms and face would feel like something was crawling on them or like I'd walked into a spider web. Sometimes I would have to wrap up tightly in a blanket to soothe it. Roberto had spoiled me and I couldn't work in this environment. Every morning I dreaded coming there, it was hard enough to come on this campus as it was. There were times I felt like the doctors in the hospital had only operated on Courtney so the students and interns could get some experience. I felt like they were dishonest and used us. I don't think I really breathed deeply whenever I was there. I just did what was necessary to get through the day. It was beginning to take so much energy mentally and physically that by the end of the day I could barely make it to my car.

***

A few days later I met with Dean Jones in her office and she mentioned that I had a deficiency, and that is why my degree had not been released. She said I needed another math class and that I should meet with the Chemistry department head to check my transcript against the requirements for my degree. I went to the records office and requested a copy of my transcript. My heart sank, I found out what had happened. I had taken Calculus I and made a 'D' before I transferred from Pittsburgh. I decided to take the class again at TSU and try to raise my grade, but I failed it. I decided to move on to Calculus II and passed it. A few semesters later I decided to take it again, but I withdrew and decide just to keep the 'D'. Taking the class over had left me with the last completed grade.

I was even more worried because if I couldn't get a copy of my degree I would probably lose my job. I had to take this class as soon as possible. The next day I went into work and talked with Jim about the deficiency and having to take a class before my application for my degree would be accepted. He was a little wary but understanding, as long as I got it done ASAP. I told him the class was offered in the summer session in June. The problem was that the class was at 8:00 in the morning four days a week. Jim said I needed to explain the situation to Irina and get her permission to take the class.

I took deep breaths trying to relax as I walked up the stairs to the lab, put my things down, and proceeded to Irina's office. I could sense her irritation as I explained the problem I had in getting a copy of my degree. I mentioned that the class I needed was at 8:00 Monday through Thursday. I was at her mercy as I asked to arrive at work 30 minutes later.

"How long will this take?" she asked impatiently.

"Eight weeks," I answered humbly.

She said something that I didn't understand and waved her hand for me to leave. I felt like a bum. This was entirely my fault for not handling my business. I should have looked into this situation years ago and fixed it on my own time, but after so many years it didn't seem to matter. So here I was in a predicament of my own making. I hadn't been in school for over 17 years and this calculus class had been my nemesis. I had taken it three times and still hadn't got a decent grade. Maybe I had a mental block of some kind.

It had been rough working with all the tension in the air so I was beat by the end of the day. I took the shuttle out to the parking lot but there was still that hill to climb where my car was parked. I started to feel like an elephant had climbed on my back, my chest was tight and my heart ached. I was getting too stressed and too tired and things were beginning to crash in on me. I could feel the grief seeping in on the edges. I was probably going to lose my job and not be able to get another one. I looked up the hill and I felt like I didn't have the energy to make it to my car. One step at a time, I told myself. I took one step and counted, one, and kept counting until I reached the car door. It was 72 steps.

***

As I drove to pick up Kim and Casey, I thought back to my college years. I had always been a good student, one of those you would have described as smart. I was living with my Grandmother and doing well, except she and I were starting to have issues as I met more people and made new friends. I was home with her less and that was becoming a problem for her. She assumed that we were going to be companions when I came down to Nashville, and although I loved being with her, I also wanted to be around people my own age.

The summer of 1981, after my second year at TSU, my running buddy Brenda and I got jobs at the Hot Stop drive-in market and were preparing to move into our own apartment. We were your typical broke college students starting from scratch. With our first checks we rented a U-Haul and drove to a used motel and hotel furniture store and came out with the complete furnishings for our two-bedroom apartment for the affordable price of only $400. Our finances were close to the vest to say the least, but it felt good to be on my own. We both worked 40 hours a week on the 3-11 shift. There were many days we had to eat Hot Stop sandwiches or hotdogs for dinner.

Brenda was from Flint, Michigan and she was pretty resourceful. We'd go to pizza buffets and stuff ourselves and her aluminum foil-lined purse with enough pizza to last for two days. Sometimes she would call a guy who was trying to talk to her to come over to our apartment and ask him to bring us some Captain D fish on his way. They were lean times but they were fun at the same time.

When fall came the electric bill got higher and our checks were stretched even further. It was early November and unusual for Nashville but we got a big snow that stranded us at the apartment and we were starving.

"Why don't you call that guy you met in the summer, the one that we saw at the club last weekend and ask him to come over for dinner?" Brenda asked me.

She knew he had a good job at Nashville Electric Service and probably had the money to feed us. I had met Cornelius in July, a few months before we moved to our apartment, and we had gone out to the movies to see Superman. He wanted me to go to his place after the movie and I thought that was moving just a little too fast. He hadn't called me back so I guess I was too slow for him. Nevertheless, we were hungry and didn't like missing meals so I called him. Cornelius was surprised to hear from me and thought my offer was pretty amusing, but he was game. Somehow he made it to our apartment in the snow but he thought it would be better for us to walk to the store instead of driving back out in the snow and getting stuck.

We trudged along in the snow talking, getting to know more about each other than we had on our date. When we got to the nearby grocery we bought all the things Brenda had asked us to get, some pork chops, Rice-a-Roni, and broccoli. Brenda was happy to cook, and later we sat down and had a good meal. We laughed and talked and had a fun and relaxed evening.

After that evening, Cornelius and I were stuck like glue. He was seven years older than I was, and it was interesting being with an older guy. I had never really dated anyone in high school and I had only talked to a couple of guys in college. I guess I was one of those girls who seems unapproachable to guys. I loved the idea that I had someone to go out with, someone to help me get home from work, and I felt protected. I would look at him and his broad shoulders as we stood in line at the movies and feel like I had a man of my own, a strong man, a grown man.

Whenever he called to go to dinner, a concert, or hangout, I was there. Cornelius wasn't in school at the time, he worked at the electric company and sold real estate in his spare time. I was trying to balance a full-time job, be a full-time student, and date very heavily. I knew I wasn't doing a very good job and that Cornelius was definitely a distraction, but I just wanted to be with him as much as I could. Most of the time I had good intentions and took my books with me to study when we went out, but most of the times the books never got opened. I was caught up in the dating experience and I was enjoying the attention.

I was determined to stay on track even with semesters where I had to withdraw from all my classes. They were other semesters when I realized that working full-time was defeating my purpose and I had to quit my job. I lived with my girlfriend from Las Vegas for a while, and then I moved in with Cornelius and buckled down to finish what I had started. After my second senior year I finally had the necessary hours to graduate. I had even found a job out of state and was anxious to move on to the next phase of my life.

I filed my paper work for graduation at the end of the semester and left to start working at Sunshine Chemical in Pennsauken, NJ. When my diploma didn't come I thought I must have a balance. I didn't have much money so I put it in the back of my mind, and that's where it had stayed until Jim told me I need to bring in a copy of the diploma.

***

The next day during lunch I went to TSU to meet with the head of the Chemistry Department. His name was Mohammad Kerem, a handsome and mellow voiced Indian man who made me feel like everything would work out fine. He said they would need the catalog for the year I came in to compare against my transcript and he didn't have one. Dr. Kerem suggested I go over to the library to find one.

At the library, I went up to the gentleman at the information desk.

"Can you tell me where the past TSU catalogs are located?"

"In the archives on the third floor," he responded.

When I got there I was embarrassed to tell the librarian that I need a catalog from 1980. Thankfully, she found one and copied the information from the Chemistry Department section for me to take back to Dr. Kerem. I dropped it off at his office with his receptionist and headed back to Vanderbilt.

The atmosphere at work was getting more hostile. Irina snapped at me for no reason and informed me that I needed to move from my desk and bench because she had a new post-doctoral person joining the lab and she wanted him to have that area. That was totally out of order, but I wasn't in a position to complain. I moved all my solutions and cleaned off the desk and bench and did my best to get through each day without causing any more upset for her or myself.

Each afternoon on my way home I counted the 72 steps to my car and prayed to the Lord to give me the patience and the strength to keep moving. Dr. Kerem called after a few days and told me what I already knew, that I would have to take the Calculus class, he also said that I was short one Physical Education credit.

"Is he serious?" I asked myself, "Really, a PE class?"

I told Cornelius about it that evening.

"Just do what you have to," he said.

I kept picturing myself in a class of students 20 years younger than me taking PE, and it was just a tad bit humiliating. Looking at the available classes offered for PE, I decided to take Yoga, surely I could do that. I had to apply for readmission before I could register, but that wasn't a problem. I registered for the two classes and used a credit card to pay the tuition bill at the bursar's office. It was official, I was back in school.

***

I was preoccupied the whole weekend before the classes were to begin on June sixth. I started to try and psyche myself up for the challenge and I had come up with a plan. I was going to listen intently to every lecture, take notes, and study my butt off. I could do this. I just needed to stay focused. Kim and Casey kept asking questions about why I was going back to school and what I was going to study. I didn't have the guts to tell them the whole story. As I sat in church that Sunday I prayed that the Lord would help me to get through these classes, and grant me the knowledge and understanding to learn this math, I was desperate.

On the morning of the first day I was nervous getting dressed. I had a long day in front of me. The school year had come to an end for the girls and they were in their summer program. I dropped them both at Fisk's mini-college, Casey was participating and Kim was a volunteer peer counselor. TSU and Fisk schools are in close proximity to each other so it didn't take long for me to get on campus. The calculus class was located in the Boswell Building which was also the new Chemistry Department's facility. When I found the room number I was nervous about where to sit in the classroom. I didn't want to seem out of place or be the oldest one there. I decided to sit in the third row, not too far in the back and not to close in the front to be conspicuous.

As the students continued to come in most looked pretty young and I wondered how I looked to them. There were a couple of people who looked like they were in their 30s and maybe one who looked around my age. One of the women who looked to be around 35, dressed nicely in office attire, struck up a conversation with me.

"I work for an engineering firm and this is my first class," she said. Hopefully going to school will help me move up to a better job."

"I work at Vanderbilt and this is my last class," I said, "I need to get my degree ASAP."

"I wish I was in your shoes," she said.

I smiled to myself, if she only knew.

The instructor, Dr. Poland, seemed too young to be a professor. He was white, possibly between 28 and 35 years old and looked like a studious nerd type with horn rim glasses. He had short dark hair and was tall and slim, just under six feet. Very personable and relaxed, his approach was no-nonsense, if you come to class and do your homework, you'll be fine. That was music to my ears as he passed out the syllabus and began his lecture.

I noticed two students in front of me that appeared to be a couple based on their body language and the fact that she was the only one taking notes. They were both small and petite and looked like they might be from the Philippines. Under their chairs were manuals for a class to teach manicures at a cosmetology school. Most of the students in this class were engineering students so I thought maybe they were going to work in a nail shop to pay their way through college.

I took down all the notes from the board and listened intently to every word. So far so good. Some of it was familiar as I concentrated and followed along with the example problems. Before long, the class time had ended and it was time to go to work. I walked to the car feeling more encouraged. I had made it through the first day.

As soon as I got to work Irina stormed out.
"Have you gotten your degree yet?" she asked in a huff.
I took a deep breath and said, "No, this was just the first day."
She turned on her heels and went back into her office.

Each day was an effort, but I refused to let her get to me. I started bringing my walkman to work to keep me mellow through the day. The new Kem CD was definitely what the doctor ordered as his melodious voice smoothed over the sharp edges of the workday. I was still following my formula in my Calculus class and I was starting to get a kick out of it. I couldn't believe it but that class was one of the more enjoyable parts of my day.

Later that week, the post-doc from California had arrived. He was average in height, pale for someone who had come from California, had sandy brown scruffy hair and grey-blue eyes, and looked tired. His name was Slava, and he was Russian like Irina, so I thought maybe he'd fare better with her than I had. He took the spot where I had sat and we talked and became acquainted. He had a wife and a new baby and they had travelled with him and they were looking for an apartment close by. I suggested that he look on Hillsboro Road because it was close and convenient to the mall. Irina saw us talking and asked him to come into her office. Fine with me I thought to myself, it was time to go home anyway.

As I trudged up the 72 steps to my car I thought about my first yoga class that evening. I couldn't wait to get there, relax, and get my Zen flowing. After Kim and Casey were settled down after dinner I drove back to the Gentry center on campus with my yoga mat in tow. Most of the students were young women in their early twenties except for a couple of white guys who were undoubtedly gay and one black guy. Several of the young women and one of the guys were more than a little over weight so I thought I should be able to do at least as well they could.

The instructor walked in, not at all what I had expected. He was an older white man with a full head of gray hair wearing large glasses. About 5'10, he was in good shape with very muscular legs. He asked us a few questions to see what knowledge we had about yoga, which turned out to be not much. He said we would begin with some simple poses that are called the sun salutation.

While following his movements and poses, my brain received the news flash. You had to be strong or in some physical shape to do yoga. I liked to walk, and we had recently bought a treadmill that I used somewhat regularly when I didn't get out, but I didn't have much upper body or arm strength. We were moving slowly, but most of the class was either out of breath or sweating by the end of the lesson. Finally he got to the part where we laid quietly on the floor and visualized that peaceful place as we relaxed every muscle and breathed from the diaphragm. That had been a real workout but I felt good and refreshed as I walked to the car. This yoga class turned out to be something I really needed.

I was keeping up with the calculus class and things were not as foreign as they seemed nineteen years ago. I was staying focused and doing all the homework problems he assigned, which was practically all of them at the end of the chapter. I was getting the answers right, at least after a few tries. Then Dr. Poland made the announcement that I had dreaded hearing, that there would be a test next week.

"Lord have mercy," I whispered to myself as class was dismissed.

Chapter Seven

Out of the Frying Pan

When I got to work, Jim wanted to meet with Irina and me together as the end of my ninety day probationary period was coming to an end. In the meeting, Irina's face was as red as her hair as she sat very agitated and upset.

Jim said, "Karen, Irina is not very happy with your work performance and doesn't think that you two can work together, what are your feelings, do you think that you two can work this out?"

I thought about how she was unhappy with everything I did, how I refused to wash the walls, how I labeled the tubes unclearly, I stacked the boxes wrong, and the order of the plates in the incubator was not how she liked it.

"No, I don't think we can," I heard myself say.

"Well alright," Jim said, "Since you both agree, why don't you take the remaining two weeks to get the new post-doc acclimated, finish out your experiments, and then turn over your notes."

That was it. Irina got up after that and left the room without a word.

"I want to thank you for your understanding and working with me on everything," I said to Jim as I walked out behind Irina, who never looked back.

I was exhausted in every way by the end of the day. I was going through so many emotions. I was upset over losing my job. I started feeling like a victim again and I hated that. I had lost control again. It seemed like the harder I tried, things kept falling apart. Riding on the shuttle to the parking lot I felt the hot tears swelling up in my eyes. I opened my eyes wider to give them more space as I tilted my head back. At the parking lot, I stepped down off the shuttle and closed my eyes and felt the liquid heat spill down my face. I looked up the hill and started walking, counting each step and then the numbers meshed into a prayer, much more accurately, a plea to the Lord.

"Help me, Jesus," I said over and over and over again with each step. "I am so tired and I am so sad." I cried to Him as I had once cried to my own father. "I don't want to do this anymore Lord, make a way out of no way, Lord. Open a door for me, Lord," I prayed out loud. "Make a path for me, Lord." I felt so desperate when I said, "Just open a window for me Lord and I'll jump out of it. I need you, Lord." I prayed and cried as I walked those 72 steps. I must have been a sight to see, a crazy woman talking to herself. I didn't want people to look at me and feel sorry for me. I didn't want to keep feeling like a victim. I prayed the Daily Prayer that said, "Bless me to let my light so shine before those around me, that they will see Your good work through me, and glorify You, O Lord."

When I got into the car I sat for a moment. I pulled it together before I drove to pick up Casey and Kim. I felt drained and numb again after we got home and I spent the evening as a couch potato. When was I ever going to get on the smooth side of the mountain?

The next morning, I told Cornelius what happened at work and he tried to make me feel better by saying that I didn't need to worry, I deserved to be treated as a professional and we would be fine. That wasn't much comfort to me knowing that we had already booked a family cruise to the Caribbean for the end of July.

"There are always other jobs," he said.

I thought about that between the few hours that I slept that night. Surely I don't have to work in a research lab for the rest of my life. I decided not let it bother me and to have a good weekend with my family.

The next week went pretty smoothly. Irina was ignoring me

as she began to train the new post-doc and that was fine by me. I was focusing my mind on my Calculus, studying my notes and working the homework problems.

On Thursday morning, I felt as if I had done all I could to prepare for the test, but as I walked towards the Science building my heart starting beating so fast I thought I was about to have a heart attack. "Oh my goodness," I said, rubbing my chest, "I have got to relax." I kept thinking about the other times that I thought I was ready for an exam only to sit down and go completely blank once I received the test paper. I started praying, "Oh Lord please help me as I take this test, help me to relax. Lord, help my mind to stay open where I can recall what I have learned."

My whispered prayer became silent as I got to the building and walked into the classroom. From the expressions on the faces spread across the room it was evident that I wasn't the only one nervous. You could almost hear a pin drop as the exam was passed out. I could feel my hand shaking as I held my pencil waiting for my test paper.

When I got mine I decided not to look at the whole test before I started. I wanted to take each problem one at a time. I took one of the cleansing and relaxing breaths that I learned in my yoga class and then I looked at the first problem. I was confused because the typing or the font made the problem look a little foreign to me, and I didn't immediately recognize what it was asking. I decided not to waste too much time on it and to just come back to that one later. The next two problems were similar to those assigned in the homework so I felt confidant while I worked them. I was feeling like this might not be one of those disasters from the past as I took my time writing each problem, writing down each step, actually finishing it without feeling like I guessed the whole thing.

Quite a few of the other students had finished after the first hour and less than half of the class was still taking the test, I was in that group, and that's always nerve-wracking. "Well, they're younger and quicker," I said to myself. When I had worked my way through the remaining pages, I turned back to the front page and now it seemed so clear about what it was asking. I finished that problem and felt relieved, I had gotten through it. I had finished every problem without drawing a blank on any of them. I turned in my paper and walked out of the science building thinking that I had at least made a 'B' or close to it.

A few students had gathered out front and were discussing the exam. One tall slim young lady with a teeny weeny afro was speaking to the guy who sat one row up and to the right of me.

"I don't think I did too good," she told him with a worried look on her face.

"Aw, it was easy," he said, "Almost too easy."

Hearing him say that made me mad. "There's always one in every class," I thought as I walked across the parking lot to my car, "A 'smart booty' who gets on everybody's nerves."

When I got to work, Irina was stomping through the lab complaining about something as the new post-doc followed her. They spoke in another language, Russian or either German. The only words that I could understand were when she turned to him and pointed her finger in his face saying, "Nicht Nicht Nein Nein," and I knew that wasn't good. I felt for him as she denigrated him in front of me and another student. He had come all the way from California and uprooted his family to be treated like this. I didn't know where I was going or what I was going to do, but I was glad I only had one more week to work there.

Later that afternoon when Slava came back into the lab, our eyes met and there was a look of understanding. He understood why I was leaving and I understood the situation he was in having a family to care for. The next morning I decided to take the day off and make it a long weekend to get my head together, what harm would it do, she couldn't fire me.

The long weekend was just what I needed. The sermon on

Sunday was about the times when we are at the end of our ropes. Pastor Drumwright said, "Tie a knot and hang on." I had to shout Alleluia on that, I had been hanging onto my rope for a while now.

On Monday morning after getting the kids dropped off and rushing to my calculus class, I could feel anxiety stirring in my stomach upsetting my breakfast as I thought about getting my test paper back. When Dr. Poland walked into the room I knew the moment of truth had arrived.

"Did everyone have a good weekend?" he asked humorously as he smiled at us.

Nervous laughter spilled across the room and then faded out as Dr. Poland began calling our names and handing the test back. I tried to gauge the reactions of the other students when they got their test paper back as I tried to sneak a look at their grades. Then Dr. Poland called my name and I raised my hand to receive the verdict. He walked over and handed me the test and that's when I saw it, the number 93 in a circle with the words "Good Job" at the top. I couldn't believe it. I hadn't made an 'A' on a math test since the ninth grade. I could have jumped up, shouted, and run clear across campus from the joy of this moment. I had done something that I never thought I could do. Before I lost it completely I took a deep breath and contained my emotions and held my lips together lest the biggest goofiest smile be pasted across my face. I caught a glimpse of Smart Booty's paper as he held it up; he had made a '96'.

Once all of the papers had been handed out, Dr. Poland said, "For you who did not do so well, it's not over, and you can get it together. For those of you who did do well, don't go getting all cocky thinking I got this."

I slid my paper in the back of my notebook and as Dr. Poland continued with his lecture. I concentrated even more, I certainly did not want to make the mistake of being cocky. I couldn't wait to tell Cornelius about my test grade even though he thinks I'm so smart and doesn't understand that this is a serious challenge for me. You couldn't tell me anything for the rest of the day. When I got to work and saw Irina, I even gave her a smile. In a way I felt sorry for these types. In all their efforts to police their employees they aren't any more productive and they make themselves even more miserable than the people working for them.

    The next morning I felt good preparing to go to class, even a little excited, not the dread I felt when I was young. I was beginning to see how our attitude about a task can have an influence on our success. When I got to class there were at least seven students missing from the previous day. There are always some who drop a class after failing the first test. Among those missing in the class included the young lady who talked about how hard the test was and the woman who worked with the engineering firm. I knew when we talked that first day that this was definitely not the first class to take when you're starting college, it could be a real confidence breaker. I was even more determined to keep up my formula for passing this Calculus class.

    At work, I spent the next few days showing Slava the ordering system and Irina's method for labeling, and where most things were stored. He expressed how temperamental Irina was and I could see he was having second thoughts about taking the position. I told him that I hadn't been able to figure out how to get along with her and the best advice I could give him was not to wait too long before he began to look for another post-doc position. For my own job search plans I had decided that I would wait until I was more than halfway through the class before I would begin to look for another job. I was eligible for unemployment and it would help me pay the bills while I focused on getting the highest grade possible in the calculus class.

    Because it was summer, Kim had a break from swim practice and she and Casey both had breaks from their ballet and tap classes. This gave me more free time in the evening to work the homework problems. Dr. Poland assigned practically all of them in the back of each chapter, but I was cool with it. I was really getting the hang of this math thing. I discovered that there were rules and steps to follow when solving problems, if I would just stick to them I could answer the problem. I learned patience as I worked through long problems, to not stress how many steps it took to get the answer. Just do them and feel the sense of accomplishment when after one page of writing you turn to the back of the book and find you have the correct answer. I wondered why I couldn't have done this nineteen years ago.

At Thursday's class, Dr. Poland announced that there would be another test next week and the chapters it would cover. The summer sessions were short and didn't leave much time to dwell on one test before it was time to take another. Here we go again, I thought to myself on the way out. I went through the motions at work, tuned in to Kem on my CD player, and the day rushed by. I felt renewed and at peace as I went through the sun salutation in yoga class that evening, almost glad that I had been required to take another PE class. It was hard and a little painful, but it felt good to use muscles that I hadn't used in a while. Now I knew why people who took yoga were in such good shape and it wasn't just deep breathing and meditation.

That Friday morning was my last day at work and surprisingly it was full of emotions. I spent most of the day going to say my goodbyes to a number of people I had worked with and had known for many years. Several people asked me what I going to do next, but I had no idea. I dodged the question saying, "I'm just going to take a break for a while." At the end of the day I turned in my work ID and keys to the lab to Jim. I knew I wouldn't miss working here in this lab or on campus, yet this Vanderbilt University and the Medical Center had been significant in many stages of my life.

My father had been saved from death when his brain surgery had finally been performed at Vanderbilt Hospital. As children we had always been told that my father was the first black to graduate from the Vanderbilt Divinity School. I was also born in the Vanderbilt Hospital, and my three children were born there too. I had worked for more than ten years in medical research here, and now I was leaving, hoping to never have to come back. I had been here for the highest and the lowest points of my life and I was ready to move on.

Those 72 steps up that hill to my car had become a place for me to pray and listen for guidance, however on this day I wasn't heartsick as I had been on so many other days, I was full of hope. I was closing a chapter in the book of my life and it reminded me of Pastor Darrell's words on many Sundays, "The best is yet to come." I asked the Lord to order my footsteps and show me that path in which he would have me to go. I thanked the Lord for bringing me to this point, for carrying me through the difficult times, healing me, strengthening me, and covering my family. I started singing, "I don't believe he brought me this far to leave me." I didn't know what I was going to do or where I was going to go. I had no plans of my own and I couldn't think past the day that I was in, and it was okay.

Chapter Eight

Turning The Page

I picked up the girls and when we got home I applied for unemployment benefits on-line. It did feel a little odd over the weekend realizing I didn't have a job to go to on Monday, but I decided to take this opportunity to do some house cleaning and painting, get in better shape, and lose some weight for our vacation.

On Monday morning I dropped the girls at their summer programs and went to class. I was keeping up and studying every day. However, there's still a little depression that sneaks in when you don't have a job, there are moments when you feel like a failure or the weakest link in the house. I didn't want my mistakes or shortcomings to put a financial burden on my family. I had changed jobs twice in the last six months and I felt bad about it, but I was doing the best I could. I kept telling myself to stay cool and relaxed and not to get emotionally undone or stressed out. I didn't want to start itching again or have my hair falling out. I spent the afternoons after class walking on the treadmill as I read my text and reviewed my notes, and in the evenings after dinner I worked on my homework problems.

On Thursday morning I was just as nervous about the second exam as the first one, I was afraid of blowing my 'A'. What if the first test had been easy like Smart Booty said, 'too easy,' and now we were going to get the real deal. I knew I had done the work, I'd studied, I'd prepared. So I starting praying for my mind to stay open and not block or go blank. I spent the whole drive over to Fisk silently encouraging myself while the kids were in the back seat chatting. After I dropped them off I started speaking out loud.

"You can do this," I said over and over, "You are intelligent, and you are ready."

I kept doing my affirmations all the way into the classroom until I took a seat. Dr. Poland walked in and greeted the class in his usual way with that knowing half-smile. He handed out the exam in that familiar silence that's always present before a test. I repeated my same strategy, tackling each problem one at a time. Taking whatever time, steps, and paper I needed to complete it, and moving to the next one whenever I got stuck. You always feel a little strange when the first group finishes and leaves and you still have a lot more to do. The initial pressure that had subsided began to rebuild. When I finished the exam, I went back and reviewed all of my answers and I felt pretty confident. When I rose to hand in my paper there were about four people left in the room. Once again I was able to complete the whole test before the class was over and nothing seemed foreign to me, most of the problems had been similar to those we did in class and on the homework assignments. I was happy and relieved. This was a good way to start the weekend.

I still had those feelings of inadequacy about not having a job at the time. If I had heard it once, I had heard it a thousand times by my mother, "always make sure you are able to take care of yourself." I had been raised to work. I had made so many decisions in my life based on how it would help me get a job. I could see that so much of my self-worth was tied up in the idea of working and how much money I was making. I didn't think that it was correct, but it's hard to change ideas that have been ingrained over a lifetime.

I decided to try and be useful by spending the long weekend painting the laundry room while Cornelius worked in the yard. It turned out to be a bigger job than I thought and I wasn't able to finish. Our weekends were basically routine, as much as I talked to Cornelius about doing things as a couple to break the monotony, he preferred to use the weekends to wash the cars, cut the grass, and whatever other work he could find. That was one of the reasons why I look forward to our vacations so much.

On Monday morning, I dropped the kids off at mini-college and went to face the music of Calculus and the return of the second exam. Dr. Poland gave the class that "Hello" that's accompanied by his half-smile that could be interpreted in more than one way. The grades were either very good or very bad as he began calling out our names to hand back the test. At first I was very anxious to see my grade, but I quickly began having second thoughts as Smart Booty was handed his test paper and I saw it was a '63'. "Oh no," I thought, what had gone wrong. My heart skipped a beat as I heard my name called. I reached out my hand and took a quick look, it was a '96'. My hands started to shake. I guess it was the excitement or the sheer joy of the moment. I had made another 'A, Good Job' and I was beside myself. This was unprecedented for me. I had always been a good student in school before college, most of the time making the honor roll. No subject had given me problems except for math.

***

I lost my confidence for arithmetic when I was in elementary school. It happened the year I was skipped from the 2nd grade to the 3rd grade halfway through the year. Because of that mid-year switch, I never learned to do long division and spent the rest of my years in school estimating and using multiplication to solve division problems. I never learned how to do it until I was grown with a child of my own in 3rd grade. When Courtney brought her math text home and needed help with her homework, I read the textbook and taught myself so I could help her. That's why it was so amazing for me to have broken through that wall of being average or less than in math. I was 'acing' exams in a calculus class where I had barely even made a 'C' on a previous test? Even I had to say, "Wow!"

Once I had absorbed the moment and settled down, I couldn't

help but feel Smart Booty's pain as he continued to stare at his test paper wondering what happened. He was so shocked by his low grade that he held the paper up to eye level in disbelief, not even caring that everyone in the room behind and to the sides of him could see his grade. Everyone else had already discreetly put their exam away. Even as Dr. Poland began his lecture Smart Booty couldn't stop looking at the test paper, he couldn't believe it anymore than I could believe my own.

At dinner that evening I was animated as I described the whole scene at the table and we all laughed when I added, "He must have gotten all cocky, thinking I got this." I was just so proud of myself. I had come back and conquered that foe that had beaten me down on more than one occasion.

I was developing a new perspective on my learning ability as I thought about all the decisions I had made in my life based on what I thought I could do or what I could learn. I had chosen to major in Chemistry as a freshman instead of Chemical Engineering even though they had more job prospects and higher pay because I didn't think I could pass the difficult math in the engineering classes. There were many other instances where I determined what I couldn't do without even trying, thinking I wasn't smart enough. I was now realizing that I could have learned anything. Nothing had been holding me back except for my lack of confidence and the realization that hard studying is rewarded.

I was halfway through the calculus class and I had an 'A' average. I was going to pass this class so it was time to start looking for another job. My unemployment check was holding off the wolves for the time being, but at $275 a week it wouldn't last. I was determined to get out of research and do something else for a while. After all, I was an intelligent person and there are many things that I could do beside work on a bench in a lab. "I have a lot of qualifications," I said to myself in the mirror as I got dressed on the following Monday. I planned to go to the employment office to see what jobs were available after class.

I had my 'I'm going to get a job' face on when I got to the unemployment office near my house in Metro Center. To my surprise and further disappointment it was slim pickings in the job market. There wasn't much to look at in any field and most of the salaries were low. I saw a poster on the wall that said UPS (United Parcel Service) was hiring and I had heard that they usually paid well so I decided to apply. They had flexible hours, the location was close to the house, and the physical part of the job went along with my goal to get in better shape. The job notice said to apply in person and that's just what I was going to do on Thursday after class.

***

Right on schedule Dr. Poland announced our third exam for Thursday of the next week, the summer schedule was accelerated and so were the speed of the tests. However, he wasn't the only one with an announcement to make, our vacation was fast approaching and I needed to be out of class for a week. We had planned it months before I even knew I would be back in school and certainly before I thought I would be without a job. I had a lot to think about. The trip had already been paid for and I hadn't bought the insurance that would allow us to cancel it, but on the other hand I had worked so hard in my class that I didn't want to do anything to jeopardize my grade. There was another test coming and the final exam and I really couldn't afford to miss a week of class lectures.

I also never wanted to take opportunities for precious family time for granted. All during class I kept thinking of how I could get excused from class, what should I tell Dr. Poland? I couldn't say, "Dr. Poland I'll be missing four days of class because my family wants to go on a cruise." That would sound crazy. With that explanation I wouldn't even excuse myself. I didn't want to just disappear and miss the week and then come back and say that I was sick. I wasn't really superstitious, but there are some things I don't like to play with. After my brainstorm I decided to tell him that I had to go to a family reunion out of town. Most people understand family obligations more than a leisurely vacation in the middle of the semester.

    I lingered after class to state my case.

    "Dr. Poland, my family reunion is scheduled for the week after next, and I'll be missing most of the classes that week. I just wanted to talk with you and see if that would be a problem."

    "Hopefully it won't be a problem for you," he said, "I can give you the homework assignments that the class will be working on next week."

    "Thank you so much," I told him, "I'll definitely keep up."

    That was a relief and one less thing to think about as I drove to UPS to put in my application.

    Pulling in to the parking lot at UPS I saw the arrow that pointed to the human resources office with applications underlined on the sign, at least I knew where I was going. When I walked into the office I was given an application on a clipboard and directed to go into the next room. Here I go again I thought as I looked around the room, most of the applicants were young black males with a few females mixed in, and I was the oldest one in the room. When did I get to be so old that I felt like a senior citizen everywhere I went? I guess forty is not the new twenty.

    On the front page of the application there was a letter that said that applicants must be able to withstand hot and cold temperatures, stand on their feet for long periods, and be able to lift 75 pounds. The list was a little daunting but I should be able to do it. Not every package would be that heavy I told myself. After I turned in my application I was told that we would have a short interview and then have a strength test. A strength test, uh-oh, I was not prepared for that. In the interview I was speaking to a white gentleman who was about ten years younger than me telling him about why I wanted to work for UPS.

After we finished talking he led me over to a crate weighed down with metal inside of it and asked me to lift it up to my chest. I guess this was the strength test they had warned me about. Okay, I tried to keep a straight face like this was something that I did several times a day. I didn't know if I could lift 75 pounds or not, but I did know that you are supposed to kneel down and lift the weight with your legs and not with your back. So I squatted down as I grabbed the crate and lifted it up to my chest for one second and then sat it back down as carefully as I could. I was surprised myself that I didn't drop the crate with a big bang to the floor like the weight lifters in athletic competitions after they complete their lifts. The guy thanked me for coming and said they would give me call.

"Karen," I said to myself as I walked to my car, "You are doing it girl." I felt like I was getting some control back in my life. I had applied for a new job and I had lifted seventy-five pounds of dead weight up to my chest.

After picking up Kim and Casey and getting their dinner together I bounced on to yoga class. It wasn't a full summer session class so this was our last lesson. Yoga had turned out to be more of a challenge than I thought it would be, but it was fun and good for me mentally and physically. I found that I was a lot more flexible and in better shape than some of the students half my age and that made me feel good. I was going to miss it and I thought that maybe I might take some more yoga classes whenever my life got settled again. We had a short written report that we had to hand in, and at the end of class our instructor asked if any of us thought we would take more yoga classes and I raised my hand.

That night I told Cornelius about applying for a job at UPS and told him about all the young guys and how I was able to lift the 75 pounds. He laughed like I was doing a comedy routine while I told him the story.

When I got finished he said, "Karen, do you really think they are going to hire you? They don't need somebody who can lift the weight one time and then sit down, they want somebody who can do that all day, walking back and forth on those trucks in the heat and when it's freezing."

I thought about that and then I had to laugh too. That was one phone call I shouldn't wait to get. The next day I went on campus to submit my application for graduation with the Chemistry Department and the undergraduate school and check for balances at the bursar's office. This time I was going to follow through on every step of the process.

***

We spent the weekend preparing for the cruise, this was our second one with the kids, and contrary to popular belief it is one of the most reasonably priced vacations for a family besides visiting relatives. Unlimited meals and entertainment are included in the price. Saturday would be a big shopping day as we checked off the list of items that anyone of us might be missing. It always got everybody excited about the trip even though I had no business being in the mall as an unemployed person. From our previous experiences, you need at least two changes of clothes for each day of your vacation, underwear included, formal wear and swim wear, and workout clothes. Not to mention the sneakers, sandals, flip flops, and dress shoes.

I was still taking notes, studying, and doing my homework for my calculus class knowing it wasn't over until the fat lady sings. I did notice that I was starting to get the cold shoulder from several of my classmates, and when I walked into the classroom early it sometimes got quiet. It was nearing the end of the semester and students were getting panicky.

One student asked Dr. Poland, "Are you going to grade us on a curve?" To the obvious dismay of a few present in the room Dr. Poland answered by saying, "No it's not necessary." From a few hard looks, I thought maybe some were blaming me. I had never told anyone my grades and I put my test papers away as soon as I saw the number at the top. I felt for my fellow students, especially for those who were struggling. I had been there and I knew that a lot of it was the bad decisions we all make when we are "young and dumb." How many times has it been said, "If I knew then what I know now," and what we would have done differently.

Chapter Nine

What Can Go Wrong?

After class I walked to the office of undergraduate studies to check on my paperwork and ordered my cap and gown. I had talked about marching with Cornelius the night before and he thought it would be good for me to participate in the graduation ceremony, that it might inspire the girls and give them something to look forward to. I felt a little embarrassed being that it had been nearly 17 years later, but I thought it might be fun.

Graduations had always been a big deal in my family. I had been present at the college graduations of my older brothers and sister and I had my camera taking pictures as they walked by. I hadn't marched in a graduation since high school and that had been a disaster. I was really excited about my high school graduation. My grandmother had come up from Nashville to be there for me, and my father's secretary, Linda, who I was close to, was also coming. When we marched into the gym proudly with our light green and dark green cap and gowns I searched through the crowd until I found my family and waved. The ceremony was great. We sang *Memories* and *Do You Know Where You're Going To*, while some of the girls started to cry.

After the ceremony, we marched out and I gave a few of my friends goodbye hugs and went to find my family. The crowd was pretty thick for a while so I couldn't find them but I kept looking. I looked inside the gym several times but it had quickly emptied out. I stood outside and thought I'll just stay in one place and maybe they'll find me. Most of the graduates and their families had taken pictures outside and then left to go celebrate.

It slowly began to dawn on me as I looked around and most of the crowd was gone that my family had left also. I couldn't believe that they had left without talking to me and I could feel the tears building up. I walked the two blocks to my house with a sense of let-down that I had never felt before. When I got home no one was there and I knew it wasn't supposed to be like this. I had been to so many graduations in my family where we meet up with whoever graduated and pose for pictures and give congratulations. Why was this time so different? I just sat down in the kitchen and waited.

After about a half hour the car pulled into the driveway.

"Why did you all leave me?" I asked as soon as they walked in the door.

"We went to take Linda home because we thought you would be spending time with your friends," my mother said.

"No," I told her, "People are not spending time with their friends after a graduation, they go find their family and take pictures and then go home, but I didn't have anybody waiting for me or taking my picture."

"You don't need to be upset because we were there and we are here now," my father said in a futile attempt to minimize what they had done.

"What was the rush to take Linda home anyway" I asked, "Why couldn't you have waited a few minutes until I came out?"

My Grandmother kept telling me not to cry but the whole day, the whole graduation had been ruined for me, and my parents were refusing to see that. An apology might have made me feel better, but my parent's generation never apologized to children for anything like we do now.

***

There was a short line at the Undergraduate School with students waiting to check their status for graduation. When my turn came the receptionist told me that my name was not on the list for having clearance and I should speak with Dr. Jones to see what the deficiency was. "What the hell is wrong now?" I thought as I walked across the hall to the Dean's office and waited for my turn in another line. It wasn't too long before she called me into her office and I sat down.

"Ms. Brown you have a deficiency that you will need to fulfill before you can get your degree," she said.

"All right," I said to myself. "Before I lose it and go crazy in here, let's just rewind." It's possible that she may not remember that we went through this scenario two months ago. I explained to her that I had come to her office before the start of the semester to determine what deficiencies were present on my transcript. Further, that I had my transcript reviewed by my department as she had advised me before the summer session and had registered for the recommended classes.

"You haven't taken Public Speaking which is a requirement for all graduates," Dr. Jones responded back.

"Well," I said, "I was told by you that I needed to fulfill the requirements of the catalog for the year I was admitted, and during the years that I attended TSU public speaking was not required.

"I instituted the Public Speaking class as part of the core curriculum myself," she said.

I again reminded her that we had spoken two months prior and that our conversation was about my needing a copy of my degree, and that I couldn't continue to work without it. I again told her I was willing to do whatever I needed to do to fulfill the requirements. I had gone to my department head as she had recommended, I had gotten the catalog, they had reviewed my transcript, I had been given the class deficiencies, I had registered for those classes, and now near the end of the summer session I am told there is another class.

"I did everything you asked me to do, Dr. Jones, it wasn't totally my responsibility to spot the Public Speaking class deficiency. I asked you what classes I needed and I don't think that it's fair to add a class that was not a requirement during the years I attended. I can't afford not to be able to work while I'm taking another semester to get my degree."

"I don't know what to tell you," she replied.

"If this requirement would have been mentioned to me earlier I wouldn't have had a problem with taking the class. I came prepared to jump through whatever hoops I needed to."

Dr. Jones sat quietly for a minute absorbing my speech.

"Waiving the class for you is not a decision that I can't make alone," she said. "Give me a day or two where I can speak to Dr. Lockheed, Director of Student Affairs, about it and then check back with me."

I needed her on my side so I tried to smooth things over by telling her how much I appreciated her help and thanked her for her time.

"That's all I need," I thought to myself. I had another exam to prepare for plus I needed to pack for our trip. I felt like pitching a fit, but I couldn't allow myself to get distracted. I had to stay focused on studying for the third test. I waited two days before I went back to the Dean's office to check if she had gotten the approval for me. After I waited in line to see her, Dr. Jones said that she hadn't had a chance to speak with Dr. Lockheed yet but for me not to worry. That only made me worry more, she didn't see the urgency in my personal problem. I knew very well you can't just hope a situation will work itself out. I didn't have time for this to drag on with my being out of town next week.

"Is there anything I can do to speed up the process?" I asked.

"You can take your packet over to Dr. Lockheed's office and let him know what your problem is if you like," she replied.

I said that I would like to do that and she gave me my packet and I walked over to the administration building to speak with him on my own behalf. I told his receptionist that Dr. Jones had sent me over and sat in the waiting area. After about thirty minutes Dr. Lockheed came out and asked me what I needed without inviting me into his office. I was giving him the short version of what had happened when he cut me off and said, "We don't even go back that far, really after seven years the credits aren't even valid," and then he walked away.

I was dumbstruck and rushed back to talk with Dr. Jones before I switched into full panic mode. Dr. Jones told me that she would handle it and not to worry. That wasn't much comfort to me but I had no choice. I was in a mess and I needed her help. Thinking that all the years and classes could end up being a total waste of time and money and I could end up with nothing was more than a disaster. I decided that I would give her a few days and check back after I took my calculus exam. It took a lot of concentration not to worry about not having a degree, but it was nothing I could do about it. I just prayed about it and put my faith in the words of the song that said, "Jesus can work it out if you let him."

I decided to focus my energy on things I could influence. I spent the next two days studying while I walked on the treadmill trying to hold onto my 'A' and trying to lose a couple more pounds before we hit the road driving down to Miami. I worked math problems between washing clothes and packing, and I was getting excited about being able to get away from all the drama for a while. Cornelius had to work Friday so we planned to drive all night when he got off to get there by Saturday afternoon.

When I got to the Boswell building the morning of the test I said hello to two students in the hallway waiting for class to start. They looked at me like I had dialed a wrong number and didn't speak. When did I get to be the bad guy I wondered?

I wasn't as nervous as I was on the first two tests. I was getting the hang of this math thing. I had finally learned the language. I took my time and worked each problem completely. I didn't care if I was the last one finished and when I turned my paper in I felt like I had done well. I reminded Dr. Poland that I would be out next week and he gave me the chapters and homework problems that would be assigned next week.

One thing down, now on to the next I thought as I walked over to see Dr. Jones. When I got in to see her she said that she was still working on it but she would handle it soon. I felt nausea seeping into my stomach at her words. She probably hadn't even talked to Dr. Lockheed and from my impression of him it was not going to be easy. Walking back across campus to my car I began to feel desperate and desperate times called for desperate measures.

When I got home I called the office of the president of TSU. The administrative assistant for Dr. Johnson answered the phone, her name was Mrs. Cunningham. She was patient as I went through the long version of the events of my return to the university to fulfill my degree, meeting with Dr. Jones and Dr. Kerem, and then the new deficiency and then more meetings with Dr. Jones and Dr. Lockheed. Mrs. Cunningham listened in silence and then said, "I want you to write all of that down in a letter addressed to the president and then bring it to my office tomorrow." I told her I would be there in the morning, thanked her for her help, and sat down to write.

I wrote my heart out in that letter including every detail and conversation. When I finished the letter I went over the packing check list for all of us to make sure we didn't forget anything. The next day I went to the president's office and dropped off the letter to Mrs. Cunningham and hoped for the best. There was nothing else I could do but wait.

I picked the kids up a little early that Friday so that I could finish packing and lay down early to rest for our night drive. After Cornelius got home, showered and changed, we loaded up the car around midnight. The kids would sleep most of the trip and we figured that we would stop at a rest stop when we got tired. It was always bittersweet whenever we took vacations. I always felt sad when we first left the house, like we were leaving

Courtney out and it hurt, she deserved to be with us. I prayed the prayer for safe traveling by car out of my prayer book.

Cornelius always liked to start out driving whenever we traveled. The adrenaline from the excitement of getting on the road carried him for a while but he got tired around 3:00 in the morning. By then, the rest that I had gotten had worn off watching the white line in the road in the night darkness. We decided it was time to stop at a rest stop and get a little sleep.

I had seen so many people sleeping in their cars at rest stops for years when we were driving long distances and it seemed to be safe. Near the entrance we saw a security car parked with a policeman inside and that made me feel better about parking. There were a few cars parked but I couldn't see the passengers, so many people have tinted windows. I saw a young heavyset Hispanic woman sitting comfortably on top of a picnic bench with her toddler. It was a hot night and she probably wanted to get them both a little air.

Cornelius pulled into one of the spaces and turned off the motor, and then we leaned back and closed our eyes. After about 15 minutes, beads of sweat had come to rest on my forehead. The temperature in the car had warmed up quickly. It was still over 80 degrees in the middle of the night outside of Atlanta.

"We may need to run the motor to keep the air on to stay cool," Cornelius said.

So we rolled the windows up with the motor running and maybe got about 20 minutes of rest before the air conditioner got too cold on us. We looked at each other and I laughed.

"I don't think that this was one of my better ideas," I said, and he laughed too.

"We should have gotten a hotel," he sighed.

"That's what I get for trying to save money," I joked.

A few minutes later a young white guy who looked like a college student pulled in about two spaces over from us. He had scoped us out and I guess we looked safe enough to park next to and get some rest. We just laughed because we had done the same thing when we drove in.

It was kind of nerve-wracking trying to sleep in a van with the motor running and the last thing we wanted to do was go to sleep with our windows down and get robbed or attacked. So we alternated between running the air conditioner and cracking our windows. It didn't last too long, after a little over two hours we decided that we were too uncomfortable. We agreed that we might as well keep driving. We had managed to get somewhat refreshed, at least enough to go a bit further, and we still had a long drive ahead of us.

We talked to stay awake, telling each other stories that we had told a thousand times before, and stopping every couple of hours to switch drivers. When the sun began to rise bringing in the new day it was easier to push through our fatigue and drive further. I always liked to listen to Luther Vandross CDs during my turn at the wheel, singing along song after song, and the time and the miles flew by. We finally made it to Florida, and about 200 miles out of Miami we hit a traffic jam that gave us a chance to catch our breath. We were shooting to board the ship around noon, but it would be between 2:00 and 3:00 before we got there.

***

When we got to the cruise terminal two busloads had just arrived. Our valiant attempt to beat the crowds had fallen short again. We were sailing on the Royal Caribbean Navigator of the Seas, one of their new ships. We found out that Michael Baisden had also booked the cruise for his "Bad Boy" Tour. There were more black people sailing than we had ever seen before. It was nice to see everyone excited and ready to have a good time.

While we stood in line Cornelius kept checking his underarms for mustiness. He's a very conscientious and neat type of guy and we had been driving all night and most of the day. I kept telling him that he was fine and not to worry but he kept checking. As soon as we got through all the checkpoints and had gotten our IDs we were able to go and find our staterooms. We only had our carry-on bags at the time. The other luggage is usually delivered to your cabin later after they are checked for contraband, but Cornelius was determined to shower and change.

As the ship slowly began to depart, I stepped out onto the balcony to watch the shore line fade away while he went through his cleanliness routine. It always fascinated me, the massive size of a ship that could actually float on the water, and the infinite amounts of water, farther and deeper than I could imagine. I love the water, but it's scary to me at the same time because I could never learn to swim and I tried lessons twice. Courtney and Kim took to the water like fish. Courtney was the smoothest most beautiful swimmer I had ever seen and Kim was so buoyant that she just lay on top of the water when she swims. Casey is taking lessons now and I guess one day I'll try again.

This was one of those moments when you stop and relax and look at nature in awe and affirm that there is truly a God and He is great. The warmth of the sun mixed with the beauty of the blue sky and the voluminous white clouds that float in weightlessness cannot be an accident. I thanked God for this moment of peace and for getting us here safely. I could finally exhale for a minute.

I had brought my calculus text and notebook with me on the trip. I was determined to follow my strategy. They say if it's not broke, don't fix it, but I was going to take the evening off to recuperate from the long drive. The kids had a room right across from ours so we all could have some space and privacy.

We had learned our lesson from the previous year when we all stayed in a suite together. It was just a little too much togetherness. Only a curtain separated us when we slept, and the TV was on their side of the curtain which gave me a steady dose of Sponge Bob, Courage the Dog, and who knows who the others were. They got tired of sleeping in one bed and were irritated with touching each other, while Cornelius and I were irritated because we couldn't touch each other. Spending twenty-fours a day together had taken its toll after five days. For a longer trip of seven days I knew we had to have separate rooms.

After the safety drill we walked around the ship to see where everything was located, like the game room, and the places to eat. As we walked Cornelius told me that he didn't have any underwear in his bag.

"You're not wearing anything under your shorts?" I asked, slightly shocked and amused.

"Nope," he said.

"You are so crazy, Dad," I said as we laughed, "Walking around here with your stuff loose."

It was so good to get a break and we had a good evening at dinner and the welcoming show.

The next morning Cornelius got me up for a morning walk on the top deck as he usually does whenever we travel.

"You know you're going to eat so at least you can clear your conscience," he said.

We walked 18 times around the top deck, an equivalent of two miles and then woke up the girls to shower for breakfast. We filled ourselves up at the breakfast buffet and afterwards they went to explore the ship and spend some time in the game room while I went back to the cabin to study and do my homework problems.

I had heard that anything that you do for twenty-one days becomes a part of you and now I believed it. I didn't feel the drudgery that I had felt in some other classes, it was something that I knew I had to do and I did it. I got satisfaction from mastering each problem and it wasn't a chore. I didn't have the feelings of inadequacy, I began to feel a sense of accomplishment and it felt good. I realized that we spend more time dreading things that are difficult or that we don't want to do than the actual time it takes to complete them.

***

My favorite part of cruising is exploring the different ports, seeing how regular people in other countries with different cultures live, where they work, what they do in their spare time, what foods they eat, even their favorite candy. I'm still a city girl and I like to go into the downtown area of the cities we visit. I loved the shopping areas of Cozumel in Mexico. It had the most beautiful silver and leather items. However, there were several moments on the trip where I would freeze up and worry, "What am I doing here, I don't even have a job."

I began to weigh my own life as the ship sailed closer to the poor Island of Labadie in Haiti. I could see a few men in frail homemade boats rowing on the waters waving to passengers. They seemed so small and of no consequence against the backdrop of the ocean and mountains surrounding them. I wondered how they lived and what they thought about us.

When we disembarked, the beauty of the tropical islands stood in large contrast to the poverty of the people that inhabited them. You could feel the hunger and urgency as the people converged upon the tourists as we looked to buy souvenirs and trinkets. The prices would start at a high level and drop to a few dollars as the tourist walked away. Small groups of dancers were performing in designated areas for tips.

When lunch time rolled around the ship had prepared a meal for us and Cornelius and the girls found a comfortable and quiet place for us to eat. When I walked back to the food area to get some drinks, a young teenage boy appeared from out of nowhere and extended his hand out to me and asked for a dollar. I felt bad because I didn't have any money on me. I told him to wait there and I would be back. I rushed back to where we were sitting and asked Cornelius to give me some money to give the boy, but when I went back to the spot he was gone. I wondered if he had understood me or if I had scared him. I felt sorry inside that

I had lost the opportunity to help someone who had approached me and was in need. It made me think about the times that I am always wanting more and expecting more when there are others who are much more in need than myself. I was having one of my deep moments where I wondered what was the master plan, what are we all doing, and what will it amount to?

The days flew by and our vacation ended too soon for me, but not soon enough for Cornelius and the girls. They were anxious to get back home, Cornelius to working in the yard and around the house, and the kids to their friends and more channels on cable. I was beginning to get a new perspective on my life. I had drifted with no direction for many years, not thinking about what my purpose was on this earth, and now I wanted to know what it was. I had been through so many things and I didn't want to go backwards. I wanted to move forward, I wanted to grow not just exist. I wanted to live again. I thought again about that emotional day as I walked those 72 steps up that hill and asked the Lord to make a path for me. Something in my spirit told me that he heard me that day, but my direction was still unclear.

Chapter Ten

Jesus Worked it Out

Monday morning was confrontation time. My vacation was over and I had to face the things that I avoided for a few days. Walking across the campus to the Boswell building I was glad there were only two more weeks left in the semester, but I had to admit I enjoyed being back in school. It still amazed me whenever Dr. Poland lectured how I could grasp the concepts and work the problems. I kept wondering what made the difference. Had I finally just learned the language of math or had I just learned how to open my mind and let the information in. If I could put this in a bottle and sell it I would surely be a rich woman.

I stayed a few moments after class to speak with Dr. Poland and make sure that I was on the same page as the class. Smart Booty made it to the desk before I did, so I hung back a bit for him to finish his question. I heard him ask Dr. Poland, "What do I need to make on the final to pass this class?" I turned away because I had been there myself and I took no pleasure in hearing that conversation. When he was finished I approached Dr. Poland.

"Welcome back, Ms. Brown," he said. "The homework problems for the two chapters we covered are listed on the board."

"I have them," I said as I pulled them from my notebook and handed them to him.

It really felt good not to have to make excuses or ask for more time. I also knew that years ago in my twenties it would have been a totally different story.

My next stop was at the president's office to speak with Dr. Johnson's secretary, Mrs. Cunningham. On the walk to the administration building I mentally prepared myself for bad news. When I walked into the office I reminded Mrs. Cunningham that I had brought in the letter for a request to see Dr. Johnson.

She smiled and said, "Everything has been taken care of, Ms. Brown, just see Dr. Jones and you shouldn't have any problems."

I hesitated for a minute replaying her words in my head.

"Oh thank you so much," I said as I brought my hands to my chest, giving myself the hug that I wanted to give her.

That was such a relief. I almost couldn't believe it. Mentally I had been gearing up for World War III. I tried to walk to the Dean's office calmly without drawing attention to myself, but I had to throw a few short jabs to the air and shout, "Yes, at last." It had been a while since I had won a fight and I was pumped.

Dr. Jones gave me the mean face when I walked into her office.

"You didn't have to go to the president," she said sternly, "I told you that I would handle it."

"I know, Dr. Jones, I just got a little panicky when Dr. Lockheed wouldn't even let me into his office to talk about it. I felt like I didn't have any other options."

"I told you I was going to talk with him," she said annoyed.

"Well, I'm sorry," I said, trying to smooth things over.

As she pulled up my information on her computer I saw the long list of students with deficiencies and knew what they would all go through. Some would continue to fight it out, while some would give it up and move on.

"You're all set," she said. "You can go to the bursar's office and pay your fees and order your cap and gown."

I handled all of my business and then went to pick up the kids. "I'll order them a pizza," I thought. It has been a good day and I wanted to celebrate.

***

The next two weeks flew by and I was ready to take the final exam. I was confident. I had studied and worked a ton of problems. I had come a long way. I was more excited than nervous when Dr. Poland handed out the exam. Looking around the room I noticed that there was less than half of the students that had sat in here on the first day of class. When he handed me the exam I smiled, all the problems were familiar to me as I looked at the first page. I wasn't cocky but "I got this," I said to myself.

"Graduating seniors can get their final grade tomorrow," Dr. Poland said as we all worked silently on the test.

After I finished the exam I walked out knowing that I had done another thing that I never thought I could do and I was proud of myself. Cap and gowns were to be picked up in the bookstore so I rushed there right after the final just to get it in my hands. There was a memo and a card with my name and a number on top of the package holding my cap and gown. The memo said graduation rehearsal would be tomorrow at 4:00.

That evening I spent some time in the mirror wondering how old I looked and if I would stand out from the other students in the graduation. There certainly wouldn't be any one there that was around the campus back in the 80s, most if not all of the professors from back then had moved on in one way or another.

In the morning I tried to wait a respectable amount of time before I called Dr. Poland for my final grade, so at 11:30 I reached for the phone and dialed.

"Ms. Brown, congratulations," he said, "You earned an 'A' in the class."

"Oh, thank you so much," I responded and slowly hung up the phone before I began my crazy woman celebration through the house.

I jumped up and down and ran through the rooms yelling

"Yes" at the top of my lungs. I clapped my hands and fell on the floor hollering out, "Thank you, Jesus." It's times like this you wonder how much noise can be heard on the outside of the walls. The next day when all the graduates gathered in the Gentry Center I could see that there were different ages and people in different points of their lives, over 400 in total. I talked to some who lived at home, some single parents, some who worked full-time jobs as we waited for the practice to begin.

At 4:00, Dr. Lockheed walked in like a sergeant ready to command his army, "Oh no, not him," I thought to myself as I remembered our brief contact. He lectured the group on the proper attire and conduct for the graduates and their families and assured us that anyone who did not adhere to the rules would be escorted out of the ceremony by the police. We did a quick run through of marching in while following the directions of the tape on the floor and noting where we would be located in the morning.

"Remember who is in front of you and who is behind you," he advised us as we left.

That evening I told Cornelius to sit near the back on the left where they could see me as I joked about Dr. Lockheed's rehearsal.

Cornelius woke me up early the next morning. Dr. Lockheed had said that if you weren't in place by 8:00 you would not be allowed to participate. I put on the black shoes he instructed us to wear with a pair of black pants. When I put the gown on I didn't feel the surge of emotions that I thought I would, maybe too much time had passed from my undergraduate days, but I did like the look.

Cornelius dropped me off at the door of the Gentry Center and went to pick up my mother while the kids got dressed. As I walked through the clusters of graduates that had gathered in the corridor where we were to wait, I could sense the anxiousness and impatience in the air like a horse poised in the starting gate ready to burst forth and show his speed and prowess. Having run in a few races already I was a little jaded, knowing that at the start we all have the same great expectations, unfortunately most won't be fulfilled. I began to realize why I wasn't as excited as I thought I would be. This piece of paper I was about to get wasn't going to make a big change in my life as it would for so many standing beside me.

    An official of the ceremony rushed through the corridors telling everyone to get in place and prepare to march in. As I got closer to the entrance into the arena I could hear the familiar tune of Pomp and Circumstance and I felt proud to be in this group of graduates. I don't remember much of the ceremony as my mind wandered. I looked up at the people in the stands waving and taking pictures and the murmur of all the whispered conversations among the graduates seated on the floor. I found Cornelius, my mother, and the girls seated far ahead to the front on the right and we waved at each other periodically during the ceremony.

    Finally it was time for the graduates to walk across the stage and receive their diplomas. It had been so long since I had the opportunity to do this and of course none of us wants to fall. I listened to all the yells and whistles as some names were called, the bull horn and screams that Dr. Lockheed had seriously warned us about, and I wondered if there would be any noise when my name was called. I heard my name as I reached the top stair of the stage and I heard the claps and cheers of my little family and I smiled from the deepest point of my heart. I crossed the stage and place my hand into the presidents' hand and accepted his congratulation with a sincere thank you. I had never met Dr. Johnson before that moment but he had helped me and I'll always be grateful for that even though he doesn't even know me.

    After the ceremony ended, I saw Cornelius in the lobby and he took my picture as I walked out and I felt like I had gotten something back that had been taken from me. Cornelius took some more pictures with my mother and me and the girls. Kim and Casey were really excited for me, and Casey insisted on wearing my cap until we got home. It was a good day and I was glad that I decided to participate. I basked in the glow of the new graduate around the house for the rest of the weekend although I had my doubts of how deserved I was.

I had learned a lot from this experience, how we limit ourselves, and I wanted to help keep someone else from making the mistakes I had made. In the Sunday paper there was an article in the paper about a shortage of math and science teachers that said if you had a science degree you could take the praxis exam and apply for a teaching position in high school. Cornelius and I talked about it and I was thinking that it might be something that I would like to do. I needed a career change and if I could keep one child from being afraid of math for their whole lives it would be worth it.

***

On Monday morning I was back on the TSU campus going to the Education Department. I spoke with the Dr. Moody about the article and asked her about the process. She pulled up my transcript and recommended that I go back to school for a Master's in Education. Dr. Moody explained that the Master's would give me the opportunity to raise my GPA while I studied for the Praxis exam and lift me to a pay grade that was comparable to what I had been making as a Lab Manager. It sounded simple enough as we talked about it, but how was I going to go back to school. Dr. Moody directed me to go to the Graduate School to get more information on enrolling.

The offices of the Graduate School and the Undergraduate School were located in the same building and right across a small lobby from each other. It was then I truly realized that something had changed. My business was now to be conducted in the

Graduate School. I asked the receptionist about the procedure for applying. She said that I needed to fill out an application and take either the GRE or the MAT and have them submitted. She gave me a catalog that would give me all the information about the graduate and their admission standards. I scanned through the catalog as I walked across campus but my heart sank with each step as I read the requirements. They were a 2.75 GPA and a 870 on the verbal, quantitative, and subject portions of the Graduate Record Examination or a 370 on the Miller Analogies Test, a writing sample, and an acceptable score on an interview.

My GPA wasn't high enough, not even with the 'A' I made in the calculus class. As I read further I saw my only hope was the conditional admission of applicants with lower grade point averages when the GRE or MAT score was correspondingly higher. If the undergraduate GPA is between 2.25 and 2.49, the GRE score must be 935 or the MAT score 383. If the GPA is between 2.0 and 2.24, the GRE score must be 1,000 or the MAT score 394. The catalog also said that those applicants seeking conditional admission must submit their MAT scores with their applications.

I promptly backtracked to the Graduate school to find out when the GRE or MAT tests were scheduled. The receptionist informed me that there was no GRE test scheduled before the fall semester, but there was a MAT test scheduled in two weeks that I needed to register for by today. She gave me a form to fill out and take to the bursar's office to pay the $65 for the MAT. I thanked her and walked away with just a small sliver of hope. Here I was still spending money and I hadn't found a job yet, and what if it's a waste of money if I don't score high enough. I knew that I had done well in the calculus class, but I hadn't been in any other classes for over seventeen years. How could I prepare to take this test in two weeks and where was I going to find a job?

Cornelius was always repeating this country saying to me whenever I had reservations about my next move, "Don't worry about the mule being blind, just keep loading up the wagon." So I went straight to the bursar's office and plopped down $65.

***

While doing my mandatory weekly job search I came across an ad in the Sunday paper about a company called Caremark that that would be opening and hiring quite a few people in Metrocenter, which was an industrial area close to the house. I've always lived in the inner cities so I have this thing about long commutes. The ad said that Caremark would pay $12.50 an hour as the starting salary which was significantly less than I had been making but it was better than my unemployment. They operated 24 hours a day and had a number of different shifts that could be worked.

Metrocenter is quiet and serene, just two left turns from the hustle and bustle of North Nashville. The buildings are widely spaced between grassy areas that are peppered with trees and knolls that surround ponds where ducks frolic as if they were in some far off meadow outside of the busy city. I thought this might be just what I needed to tide me over while I go back to school. It said to apply in person, so I planned to do that first thing in the morning. School would be starting in a couple of weeks and I needed to find a job and get things settled before I joined the rat race of dodging all through Nashville again. I decided to wear dress slacks, a little professional but casual at the same time.

"Wow," I said as I drove up. There were cars everywhere and it took a few minutes to find a parking space. Well, it seemed like the places that were hiring weren't among the best kept secrets in Nashville. The crowd was just as big inside the reception area as it was outside. I took an application from the young lady at the front desk and looked for a seat to fill it out. It's funny how people looking for jobs at the same place are careful not to make eye contact, but sneak opportunities to check out the competition whenever they can.

After I turned in my application I was sent to another waiting area where they gave a mini data entry test on the computer and then a short interview. I guess this is just a part of the process of growing older when you begin to find that you are being interviewed by people who are practically 20 years younger and less qualified than you are. I knew the routine and the script well. Afterwards I was thanked for coming by and given the proverbial send-off, "We'll call you and let you know." I'd heard that enough times to know that you don't hold your breath waiting for the phone to ring.

***

Kim's fourteenth birthday was coming up and I was feeling anxious about it. Courtney had gotten sick when she was fourteen and I had an irrational fear that something might happen to her at this age. The number fourteen has been a significant number in my life. I was born on the fourteenth of September, my Dad had passed away fourteen years after his surgery, and Courtney was born that same year, fourteen years later I lost her at age fourteen. When I looked in her wallet, there were fourteen dollars in it. Kim was also born on the fourteenth day of August and Casey would have been born on the fourteenth of May, but I asked to come in for the c-section a few days earlier. The number fourteen had been associated with more significant events in my life and I knew this would be a long year for me. I prayed the prayer for young children, "For the promise of Your Word to keep my children in all their ways and to bless them with a long, happy, healthy, safe, and Godly life."

I spent the next few days shopping for school uniforms and checking off the supply list items for the girls to go back to school. As luck would have it, the date of the MAT test would be on the first day of school, August the sixteenth. I went on the internet and googled MAT test and it said it was the Miller Analogies Test and it measures analytical ability. I looked further trying to find a tutorial or a practice test to help me prepare because I needed to do well. Unfortunately I didn't have the time or the money to take a preparation course, but one website did have a few practice questions. It looked like you needed to analyze the relationship between different concepts. How could I prepare for that anyway?

The first day of school was always hectic, but it was the first day in high school for Kim, so I knew she was going to be nervous and want me to walk in with her. Casey was going to the first grade so I knew I had to get her there by 9:00. It was only going to be a half-day and I even considered letting them miss today to make it a little easier on myself because I had to be at the testing site in the business building at TSU by 9:30. The high school report time was 7:15 and I needed at least twenty minutes to get there.

We got to Hillsboro High School with a few minutes to spare. The freshman met in the auditorium where they were given their rosters according to the first letter of their last names so they could find their homerooms. "Come on, come on, let's get moving," I whispered under my breath when we got finally got her roster. I still had a lot ahead of me. Kim and I finally found her homeroom after asking one student and then another as we got closer. She gave me a quick hug when the coast was clear. After that I ran two steps and then walked two through the hallways, repeating the cycle all the way to the car.

When I got back to the house Casey was dressed and after a quick snack we were in motion to Robert E. Lilliard Elementary School. Thank goodness it was close to the house. The classrooms for each grade were posted on the front door. I found her name on the list and rushed down the halls to the designated door. I met Casey's new teacher and made my way out as quick as I could. I had twenty-five minutes to get to the testing site for the MAT.

It was definitely an advantage for me to be familiarized with the TSU campus lately, especially today when I didn't have time to look around. I was running again and I had been running all morning. I tried to calm down some when I was just a few feet from the testing room. I walked in at 9:25. I was the last one to show up and most of the computers were taken. I found one in the back and followed the directions of the proctor to get logged on. It was the first time that I had sat down this morning except when I was speeding across the interstate driving.

I could feel the perspiration under my arms and the sweat dripping down my back as I tried to catch my breath and compose myself. I had not even had time to stop and ask the Lord to help me through this test. "Please, Jesus," I said in my head. There was a one hour time limit so I had to get started. I took each question one at a time, thoughtfully but not lingering too long. The worse thing that I didn't want to happen was to run out of time before I finished. I heard the proctor call that said, "Ten more minutes," and by the next call of "Five more minutes," I had finished. The proctor said that we could pick up our scores in the testing center on Monday. I felt like I wanted to go somewhere and collapse for the rest of the day but no such luck, Kim had to be picked up by 11:15 and the Casey at 11:45. My breakdown would have to wait as usual.

***

The rest of the week went by quickly as we settled back into our busy routine of school, the girls dance classes, and swim practice for Kim. There was only one more week to register for classes at TSU and I hadn't even submitted my application. When I got to the testing center I gave this tall dark-skinned guy who was at the service desk my name and told him I was there to pick up my MAT score. He looked into a file to retrieve the results and then he called out to a woman behind him sitting at a desk.

"Hey, Barbara, here's the one who got the 416."

The woman got up from the desk and walked over to the

counter and looked me straight in the face as if there were some revealing message to be found there.

"So you got the 416," she said nodding. "Okay, well congratulations you got the highest score."

I couldn't believe it, me with the highest score. I could hear my heartbeat again, not from fear, but from excitement and happiness. I had done it. I had a score high enough to get myself admitted into graduate school.

"Who knew, baby, who knew?"

Things were beginning to open up for me and I was ready. I couldn't wait to get over to the graduate school and submit my application with my MAT scores. Things were definitely looking up. Wait until I tell Cornelius and the girls that I am going to graduate school.

Chapter Eleven

New Beginnings

Six months ago this wasn't even on my radar, but I was finally moving in a positive direction, I had hope again. I realized that you don't necessarily have to grab the golden ring, but just having the possibility or the opportunity to keep reaching for it is very satisfying. I vowed not to waste this chance and to make the most of it.

After a week I received my conditional admission acceptance letter. I looked at the catalog and wanted to focus on the administrative aspect of education instead of the curriculum and learning side. I chose my first class, Introduction into School Administration. It would be a real juggling act, but this class was one day a week and didn't have any conflicts with the girls' dance classes and Kim's swim practice. I used my credit card to pay for the class, a bad move for someone without a job, but I refused to worry about the mule being blind.

Before the first day of class I got a call from Caremark, they wanted me to come in for the next training class starting in three weeks, but I would need to take a drug test. The person on the phone said that I would receive the paper work to take to the drug testing center within the next day or two. I felt good, things were coming together.

On the first day of my class I watched the other students walking across campus and I flashed back to my days here in the 80s, remembering how it felt to be a freshman, the newness and the apprehension of not knowing what to expect and not knowing my way around the buildings. The students looked familiar, not much had changed, and then it struck me that Courtney would have been a freshman in college this year. It should have been her walking to class instead of me. The realization gnawed at my insides and I began to hurt. She had looked forward to this day for so long and it would never happen. I could feel myself falling in that abyss of grief so I stopped myself. I had learned how to switch my thoughts before they engulfed me. Maybe it wasn't a coincidence that I was back in school, maybe it was by design. I already knew it was a divine intervention, maybe it wasn't just for me. I pictured her coming with me and going to college through me. I would do it for her, dedicate it to her, it would be as if she were going.

The atmosphere of this class felt totally different from the summer math class. I was a graduate student now and I was redeemed from my less than stellar undergraduate years and I had a clean slate. As we gathered in the room waiting for our instructor I realized that the class sizes are much smaller in graduate school. I was also surprised to find that at a HBCU college; most of the graduate students were white.

When the instructor walked in right at 4:40 it was amazing. He was a dead ringer for Burl Ives, the character I remembered from my childhood Christmas favorite, Rudolph the Red-nosed Reindeer. He had the white hair and the long beard, small glasses and the big belly. The similarities even reached into his voice, an even toned soothing quality that suggested each word had an individual importance. He introduced himself as Dr. Hullette, handed out a syllabus, and gave us a brief synopsis of his education and career. He was surely a unique character and had a varied professional life than included being a chef and managing a major a chain of hotels.

After the painstaking segment of when we all introduced ourselves, I found that most of my fellow students were already working as teachers and were pursuing the Master's degree for the higher pay scale. The majority of them had come from surrounding counties throughout Tennessee. I felt as if I had entered another world as Dr. Hullette engaged us in conversations about the role of administrators as leaders not as managers. He asked us to write a few paragraphs about our philosophy of leadership which would serve as an example of our writing style. I couldn't remember the last time that anyone asked me what I thought about anything. I began to feel more significant and more alive. I guess I was still trying to move from existing to participating in life, to having peace with myself and what I was doing.

The class lasted close to the three hours that it was scheduled for. I could see Dr. Hullette was one of those instructors who was going to give you your money's worth whether you wanted it or not. I rushed out worried about how the kids were doing without me. When I got home the girls were fine, just watching TV. Maybe I could take the time to do this after all.

The next day I received the paperwork I needed to go and take my drug test. Cornelius said they were no big deal. Drivers for MTA had to take random drug tests throughout the year. It just seemed like an invasion to me. Why do I have to take a drug test to work somewhere? What does it matter what a person does in their off hours as long as they perform well on the job? I didn't have any drugs in my system to detect, but to me it was a matter of personal freedom and privacy. Nevertheless, I needed to get back to work, so whatever I had to do, consider it done, even peeing in a bottle.

It was on my birthday that I got the call from the Caremark training representative asking me to report for training during the last week in September. Happy Birthday I had a job. In the meantime I was loving my class, the experience of discussing important issues about education, and the reading and the writing. I felt like I was growing again. Dr. Hullette addressed us all by our sir names. "Ms. Brown, what is your interpretation?" he would ask when following up on another students answer. The level of respect that was in the classroom was something that you don't always see in the workplace and it was refreshing. I was somewhat intrigued by Dr. Hullette, I felt like he had the answers to many of the questions I had about how to be successful.

The training hours scheduled for the job at Caremark would be from 6:00 to 2:30. This would work out perfectly. I would be done with my work day just in time to pick up the kids from school and get to my class. A week later on my first day I realized that I had to wake up around 5:15 to get to work by 6:30 in the morning. I had seen Cornelius leave for work in the dark for many years, and now it was my turn. It was different leaving the house before the kids were even up. The plan was for Cornelius to wake them up and take Kim to school first, pick up his work assignment from NES, and then take Casey.

It was still dark out when I left the house and there were only a few cars on the street from the short drive from my house to Metrocenter. The area looked peaceful in the day breaking hours as I found a parking spot and walked in ready for a new experience. As soon as I arrived I was given a name tag, a training manual, my own personal headphones, and a room number. I learned that the new employees would be processing the refills for prescriptions for patients under the new Medicare prescription plan put into place by George Bush.

We were divided into about four classes of about twenty-five people. Inside the classroom I found a comfortable seat close to the back but not in the last row. I leaned back in the chair and looked around at the notes posted on the walls and thought, I have a job again. After a few minutes we were introduced to our trainer, Janice, who was from St. Louis. She was very animated and spoke with her hands, which was distracting because she had the vitiligo skin condition. I found myself daydreaming from time to time as I looked at her hands for recognition of something in the patterns of her skin colorations like looking for characters or shapes in the billows of huge clouds in the sky.

During the first week of training we sat desk to desk in a row with five people in five rows. The majority of the people in the class were women, mostly black with three whites, and only about six guys. I would say most were in their thirties with children. Slowly throughout the day we all became acquainted between the modules in the training manual. We found out where everyone had previously worked before coming here, what church they attended, how many children and what their ages were, and if they were married or single. We spent eight hours plus lunchtime together each day so we got to know as much about each other as we learned about the Medicare program.

The first few days the room buzzed with the anticipation of people who had just been released from the unemployment roll. However, after a week of training most of us there had already found out that we didn't want to do this for the rest of lives. The job wasn't hard; you processed prescription refills for clients that used the mail order system, but it was monotonous. The bulk of the training was learning the language that prescriptions were written in, the drugs that were covered, and also the ones that weren't by the new Medicare D prescription program. We learned to navigate through the software and were practicing amongst each other by the second week.

I had worked as a telemarketer on a couple of jobs when I was in undergrad, so I knew I didn't like being on the phone all day, but this was just to get me by while I was in school and the schedule worked out with the kid's school hours and my class. Since we were only training the atmosphere in the room was slow-paced and relaxed. The different backgrounds and personalities in the classroom were good for many moments of comic relief throughout the day. Nashville is not a big city and several people had known each other before and had worked together on other phone related jobs at Sprint. Two people had even previously dated.

One tall and chubby guy named Matthew, who sat next to

me in training, had recently moved here from Virginia and it was hilarious to watch his attempts to make a play for most of the women in the class. He started with the most attractive one, Regina, who was way out of his league, but you had to admire his confidence. Why start at the bottom? I listened as he told her that he would love to take care of her boys because he didn't have any children, and I think she even considered it for a moment before she came to her senses and said, "I'm already seeing someone right now." Over the weeks of training he kept me entertained with his unsuccessful flirtations with at least ten women in our class until there were no single or available women left to approach in our group. Matthew wasn't deterred, he moved on to women in the other classes that we met during lunch in the break room.

***

   My daily schedule was full, getting off at 2:30, picking up the girls from school, getting them to both their tap or ballet classes and Kim to swim practice, my class on Wednesday, and writing papers on the weekend. I was beginning a love-hate relationship with Dr. Hullette. He was a little full of himself and was always revealing more of his career accomplishments but he was also knowledgeable in many areas. He kept us to the last five minutes of each class and he assigned a lot of reading and writing but I felt like I was really benefiting from being in his class. He challenged the class and picked our brains often. They say a mind is a terrible thing to waste and I realized I had been wasting mine for more years than I cared to count. Dr. Hullette had to be near or already at retirement age but he always had something on his horizon, a new venture or project that he was pursuing. I loved that about him and I wanted that for myself.

   Towards the end of the semester I began to have some problems with my hands getting cold and the tips turning blue. Whenever I would grab food items out of the frozen section in

Kroger my fingers would not warm back up. It was as if the circulation in my finger tips would shut off and it took shaking and squeezing my fingers to get them warm again. I was wondering if it was just stress from longer days but my knees and legs were bothering me some too, so I made an appointment with Dr. Sanders to get it checked out. I had to wait for about two weeks before I could take a day off from work. No one was allowed to miss any of the first phases of the training unless it was an absolute emergency. By mid-November we were ready to move to partnering with someone who was already taking phone calls outside of the training room.

The main floor where customer service workers actually took calls was in a huge room with over two hundred desks. All the employees were divided into fifteen teams. Each person had at least two people on either side or in front of them. This was true togetherness. We were all assigned to a buddy and we sat in a chair behind their desk with our head phones connected into their phone where we could hear their conversations with Medicare D clients. The job didn't require much from you mentally but there was a rigid working environment where every minute was accounted for. The number of hours we worked was determined by whether our headset was connected and if we were logged on.

We listened for about a week before we were assigned to a permanent team. It was then we were separated from the security and company of the people that we had trained with for more than six weeks. The deadline for enrollment into the Medicare D program was approaching so we would all be required to work a minimum number of overtime hours to accommodate the expected rush. Everyone would be required to work Saturdays and Sundays every weekend which were the busiest days. Holidays and the shopping season were coming so very few were upset by the additional mandatory overtime hours. It cut into my weekend study hours, but for the extra money I was going to make it work.

Dr. Hullette told us he was giving a final exam of essay questions after Thanksgiving and we also had the term paper that he specified in the syllabus. I had learned so much from my return to the classroom during the summer. Specifically, to never procrastinate. That was the evil nemesis. I had developed the habit of starting any assignments as soon as I knew about them. Gone were my days of rushing in at the last minute cramming and writing the night before a test or a paper was due. My term paper for Dr. Hullette was already completed so I just needed to keep up my reading assignments over the holiday.

Thanksgiving is always a marathon because I was usually alone in the shopping and the cooking. This year would even be harder because I would have to work the whole weekend. Somehow things all came together and we had a delicious dinner. The next day, there were even a few people at work who had gone Black Friday shopping at the crack of dawn to pick up some deals before coming in at 6:30.

Next week was the last class of the semester and we had voted to take our final exam during that class. The final was not a problem. I had gotten familiar with Dr. Hullette's way of thinking and the way that he wanted us to analyze situations. On the way to the parking lot I heard a few students say that they wouldn't take another class from him anymore but he didn't bother me. I knew I would take another class from him, he wasn't easy but he was fair. It was about ten days later that I saw my final grade on the mytsu website. I had made another 'A'. I was on a roll.

***

I had cancelled my previous appointment to see Dr. Sanders not wanting to miss a day from work, but my hands and legs were still giving me problems so I rescheduled. I recognized his nurse before she called my name in the waiting room. She always fascinated me, she was tall and slim, at least 5'10", long legs and long arms and moved quickly and effortlessly. Her body looked like a woman around the age of thirty, but from the neck up she looked like she was well over sixty. Her hair was totally white and she wore old-fashioned glasses that she let slide to the end of her nose.

After a short examination Dr. Sanders asked me if I had heard of Raynaud's disease, which I hadn't. He said that he was going to order some blood work that would tell him exactly what the diagnosis was. He gave me a small piece of paper and told me that it was one of the three things listed. I looked on the paper and read scleroderma, rheumatoid arthritis, and multiple sclerosis. I folded the note and held it in my hand as I walked out of his office. Wow, I thought as I walked to the section of the clinic where the phlebotomist worked. I had seen a very sad movie on the Lifetime Network about a woman suffering with scleroderma and I didn't want to go through that. I had also seen a documentary about a woman who had multiple sclerosis and that was also a long road downhill. I couldn't believe I was actually hoping that my tests came back with rheumatoid arthritis. After my blood was drawn, I was told it would take a couple of weeks before the results would be back.

***

My job was becoming easier and more repetitive as we got used to the usual problems. There were countless complaints from people trying to get their prescriptions refilled and the crazy calls from people who tried to get their prescriptions for oxyContin refilled before the regulated number of days. I was still on cloud nine from my grade in Hullette's class and Christmas was on the way. Christmas was still another bittersweet holiday. I enjoyed decorating the house and shopping for gifts, but I always saw something that I wanted to buy for Courtney and that would always give me a few holiday blues.

We still had to work a lot of overtime which wasn't all bad, but the work had slowed down with longer breaks between calls where you could talk to the person next to you and hear the inner office gossip. Caremark ran a tight ship and calls were monitored regularly. If you did anything or said anything to a client that was rude or out of order everyone knew it, because when it happened the person would leave the room and very shortly afterward their supervisor would come back with a small cardboard box and their personal items on the desk would be packed up and we would never see them again.

Chapter Twelve
Building Momentum

I had made some ambitious resolutions for the New Year, to take as many credit hours as I could, lose the last 20 pounds that never go away, and take another great vacation. Now that I had gotten back into school I knew I would never get finished taking one class at a time. Looking at the catalog I decided to take three classes or nine hours, and I also had to apply for regular admission, the conditional admission would not last past the second semester. The biggest problem was that I didn't have any money saved and we had to pay for the tuition with a credit card and a full load would be much more expensive.

I hated running up more bills while I was making less money, but I was determined to make it work and the overtime was coming in handy. Just when you think that you have everything worked out there are more issues to consider. When I got to work the next week there was an announcement made at the beginning of the shift. There would be no more overtime hours and hopefully they would not have to lay off anybody. There's always seemed to be a fly in the soup.

That little announcement created a great amount of tension on the floor. It was just after the holidays and people had bills to pay including me. I refused to worry about the mule being blind and went forward with registering for my classes, Instructional Leadership, Education Law, and Education Research. I went to the graduate school and applied for regular admission and made a trip to the bookstore to buy my books. The challenge had been choosing sections of my classes that did not conflict with the girl's activities. I was determined not to upset their schedules.

It meant that I had to take a weekend class that met only once per month, but it was four hours on Friday and ten hours on Saturday. The additional class work made me feel like a full-time student again and I loved it. It struck me funny that during the time when I was in school it didn't mean as much to me as it did now, and I definitely didn't get a kick out of it. I could see that the real importance and opportunity of going to college is lost on most young people.

The overtime that I had gotten used to had ended and the amount of money I earned on a regular check should have been marked insufficient funds. It was getting harder to make ends meet especially with the added tuition expenses. It was also time for each of us to get our ninety day evaluations by our team leader. During my meeting the team leader mentioned that I had nine infractions and if I reached thirteen I would have to be terminated.

"What were the infractions?" I asked her, dumbfounded.

"You have come back from lunch late more than once and have gone over the one minute allowable time that you are given to be back on the phone," she explained. "You have also gone over the one minute grace time that you have to get on the phone after you come in the mornings. You also have six minutes of personal time each day and you have gone over that amount on several occasions."

I could see that minutes were very serious at Caremark.

"I wasn't aware that I was being that careless on my time," I told her, "I will definitely work harder to make sure that doesn't happen again."

As I walked to my desk I could see the writing on the wall, I wasn't going to have a career at Caremark. It probably wouldn't be much longer before they were carrying out my belongings in a cardboard box. Everyone was quiet after their evaluations, and we all tried to gauge the expressions of our co-workers when they came out to see if the news was good or bad.

I told Cornelius about it when I got home and he laughed and he said, "That's how it is out here. You have been out of the real job market baby, that's what time it is."

Well I knew one thing, it was time for me to look for another job before I ended up being unemployed again.

I already knew there weren't a lot of opportunities floating around right now with the recession in full effect, but I couldn't believe that I needed to consider working in research again. I didn't want to get under the stress or the misery of working at Vanderbilt. I looked at the Vanderbilt job website and the long list of research assistant positions. I couldn't logout fast enough. I had been to that amusement park, seen the house of horrors, rode the rollercoasters, and had bought the t-shit. I could only hope that maybe there was a position at Meharry that I could apply for. I logged on to the Meharry website and saw two jobs that I was qualified for and applied for them both, I had nothing to lose and much to gain.

***

My new classes were interesting. In the Leadership class, my professor was from Iraq and he always made every effort to criticize his own country with such passion that it became a tad uncomfortable to hear and I didn't always agree with what he was saying. I learned about the qualities and attributes of a good leader and what the job of a leader really is. As I looked at my working career I knew many of my bosses had not ever taken a leadership class in their lives. My education research class was going to be the worse of the three because he divided us into groups of four for our semester research project, and I knew from experience that group projects are usually a disaster with one person doing all the work. I was determined that the person would not be me.

***

It was around the first of February that I got a call for an interview at Meharry and I was hopeful that it might be the opportunity to get my fanny out of the fire at Caremark. Counting the minutes and seconds for lunch and break times was a bit much for me and I was pretty sure I had accumulated a few more infractions. I probably could have disciplined myself to coming in early and leaving lunch early every day, but the money just didn't create enough incentive for me. Cornelius explained to me that when people don't have options they do what they have to do. I guess in my mind I still had options. I scheduled the interview around my half hour for lunch so I wouldn't lose much time on my steadily shrinking paycheck.

Being on the fourth floor of the Basic Sciences Building was very familiar to me. My first job in a research lab out of college was on this floor in the same department. When I got to the office of Dr. Coleman, I recognized him as the principal investigator in the lab next to my boss's lab when I last worked here in 1990. He was very close to Dr. Wilson back then and they talked regularly. I didn't mention it as we greeted each other and shook hands and I wondered if he remembered me. I also recognized him from church, we both attended the 7:30 service and that also went unmentioned.

He began to tell me about the job and it sounded like I would be working for several people so I asked him about the project. Dr. Coleman saw my confusion and said, "This interview is for the lab coordinator position in the Molecular Biology Core." He explained that he was also hiring a research assistant position but that was not the position he was interviewing me to fill. I tried to remain cool through the rest of the interview, but that was great news for me. I had tired of the lack of job security that came with working with individual researchers. You had a job as long as they had grant money and that was never guaranteed. I had changed labs many times based on grant funding and it was disruptive if you have a family and the economy was worsening.

Dr. Coleman didn't talk much and he spoke barely above a whisper. I couldn't tell what kind of impression I was making but I wanted and needed this job. I thanked him for considering me and hurried back to Caremark.

When I got seated at my desk I noticed that I had taken an hour over lunch time, not too bad for an interview and travel time included. The call volume was slow that afternoon and one of my co-workers, Shelley, turned around to talk not long after I had gotten back.

"Karen we thought you were gone girl," she said.

Then somebody else said, "We thought you got fired."

I laughed as quietly as I could and said, "Not yet, you see my little belongings are still sitting here. They didn't come and take my mug or my candy away in the cardboard box."

We all got a good laugh about that. I told them that I had gone on a job interview.

Shelly looked at me with true sincerity and said, "I hope you get the job."

I knew she meant that for more than one reason. They were still paring down the numbers of employees on the floor and everybody here was here for the same reason, they needed to work. If I got the job that was one less person that had to be pointed to the door and it increased her chances of keeping her job.

***

My classes were going well and I had received my letter of acceptance into the graduate school, it was official and it made me feel proud of myself. I was a graduate student pursuing a Master's degree. My education law class felt like I was in law school, and I got a kick out it. I had wanted to go to law school when I was younger. In the moments when my mind wandered during the long hours on Saturday during the lecture, I thought about what I might be doing if I had chosen to pursue law school.

Would I have found the money, would I have graduated, where I would be living and working? I decide that was too much to think about and I needed to focus on the here and now.

In my leadership class, Dr. Gundi, the professor, always took ten minutes to make a point that he could make in three, so whenever I answered his essay questions I always took a paragraph to say something I could have said in one sentence, and he loved it. The only problem was the research class, the three other people in my group lived outside of Davidson county so we were having a difficult time planning when to meet to plan our project. We were falling behind on our research because we had not settled on a project. It was wearing me down so I suggested that we do a health education project in conjunction with the Northwest YMCA that was located near my house and not too far from campus.

I thought I should get some information about upcoming health fairs from the YMCA so I stopped by there one day after I picked up the girls from school. The facility had grown considerably since Courtney and Kim went to the daycare there. The manager was introduced to me as Ms. Rochelle and she was very helpful. She said they were doing a health fair in about a month and that my group might like to set up a booth. I told her that sounded great. We just need to get her the information for our theme within a week. So far it seemed like I was doing all the work again, but at least we were getting something into a planning stage.

Just as I was about to get in the car I saw a co-worker from Cell Biology at Vanderbilt, Cheryl Simmons. We had become fast friends years ago, before Kim was born, after we realized how much we had in common. We both were from Philly, we both had worked at Meharry before coming to Vanderbilt, we lived about three blocks from each other, and we both had kids in the YMCA daycare. I hadn't seen her in several years since I left the Genetic Medicine Department at Vanderbilt.

It's weird how tragedies can push people apart instead of bringing them together. There were several people I had been close to over the years that had disappeared out of my life and I hadn't seen since Courtney had gotten sick. I guess it's part of people not knowing what to say or how to react. I stood at the car door bracing myself against the cold winds as she approached.

"Hey girl," she said, "I hear you're thinking about working at Meharry again?"

"I had an interview there a couple of weeks ago with Dr. Coleman, but I haven't heard from him," I said.

"Well, I saw him when I was over there for an interview myself last week with Dr. Hilliard and he told me he was trying hard to get you to come up there."

"Really?" I asked kind of puzzled. I hadn't spoken with him since our interview. "I'm going to have to give him a call. I've been waiting to hear from him."

We went through a quick catch-up on our children and then I got in the car. Dr. Coleman seemed nonchalant during the interview and I didn't think I had made a good impression. I wondered why he hadn't called me and offered me the job if he wanted me but I knew I was going to call him first thing in the morning.

When I got to work the next morning I could hardly wait for break time. I was always lagging behind the crowd in the latest technology so I didn't have a cell phone to make the call at my desk. When 9:15 came I was a blur moving down the hallway to the break area. I took a deep breath and dialed the number.

When Dr. Coleman answered I said, "This is Karen Brown, I just wanted to call and let you know that I am very interested in the lab coordinator position and I would love to have the job if you haven't filled it."

"When would you be able to start?" he asked.

"Immediately," I replied, trying not to sound too eager, "But

I would like to give a two week notice where I'm currently working."

"That will be fine," he said, "You should be hearing from the Human Resources Office soon."

"Thank you, Dr. Coleman, I'll look forward to that," I said and hung up the phone. "Thank God," I said to myself.

What if I hadn't run into Cheryl? I had gotten another much needed reprieve. I could feel another path being made for me on this journey and I was exhilarated on the inside but I maintained a cool exterior for the small crowd in the break room. This job had been a blessing for me and my family to get me to another point and I was thankful for the experience but I was glad to move on further. I didn't have time to get a snack and sit down so I celebrated by buying the super big and super fattening honey bun to take back to my desk. I vowed to only eat half of it and save the rest for Casey. She was always checking my lunch bag for sweet leftovers. I started to go into the office and give notice to my team leader but I thought I had better wait until I hear from the Human Resources office at Meharry.

***

In the meantime my blood work had come back in and I thought I should see what the diagnosis was before I started my new job. I made an appointment for Friday so I could have the weekend to think about it. On Friday morning I decided to take a sick day instead of stressing myself out trying to get back within an hour.

After I dropped the kids off at school I went to Dr. Sander's office. It seemed like a long wait to me before his nurse called my name and led me to one of the outpatient rooms. Dr. Sanders came in rushing as he normally does, sat down in the chair across from me and said matter-of-factly, "The results of our blood work say that you do have rheumatoid arthritis." I was honestly a little relieved until he continued on saying, "the range of the sedimentation classifies you as being moderate to severe." Moderate to severe, what did that mean? It was the severe part that was giving me a few problems. Dr. Sanders said that he could treat me if I wanted him to, but he recommended that I see a specialist, and he gave me the name of someone in the arthritis clinic of Centennial Hospital. Before I left his tall nurse gave me several pamphlets about rheumatoid arthritis to read at home.

    I read some of the pamphlets as soon as I got in the car and some of them were a bit frightening, but I decided not to worry about it, people lived with arthritis every day. When I told Cornelius about it he started getting on my nerves asking me a bunch of questions that I couldn't possibly know the answer to, so I told him to make sure he went to see the specialist with me on Monday. I have always gone to my doctor's appointments by myself but Cornelius's curiosity got the best of him this time and he went to the appointment with me.

    The specialist was Dr. Farrell and I didn't care for his manner, he seemed to want to tell me what medicines to take and not explain the reasons or the side effects. He wanted me to take a medicine call methotrexate, which he said was a chemotherapy agent. After he said that I was not interested. I definitely didn't want go through the side effects of chemotherapy. I decided I would find another doctor who would give me all the options, one I could be more comfortable with. I wasn't feeling really bad so it could wait. I guess I had gotten used to feeling this way and had forgotten what feeling good was like. I decided to get settled back in at Meharry and see how this new employment thing worked out.

***

    It was the end of February before the Human Resources office called me and offered me the position and it made my day, I was going back to Meharry. The administrator gave me a few dates to choose for my orientation day. I chose March 20, after

Courtney's birthday, that was an official holiday in our house and it would give me a couple of days break between jobs to make the transition. After that phone call I could finally give my notice at Caremark. I didn't care much for the job, but the people I had met made it tolerable and even fun at times. In some ways we were like a little family, I was going to miss them and I hoped that I would stay in contact with some of them.

The orientation at Meharry was informative and coincidentally, my old friend Cheryl was there starting a new job in the new HIV Department. I thought about how much life changes when you're in an academic science career. We had started here at Meharry, spent many years at Vanderbilt, and were back at Meharry again. I smiled to myself, happy about having a new beginning. After the orientation of the morning I went over to see my new boss after lunch.

Dr. Coleman was a man of few words and he showed me the work area and explained my responsibilities as lab coordinator. The only lab experiment that I would be doing was DNA sequencing for researchers and that sounded great. I had good hands and great lab techniques but I had my fill of working on the bench. Dr. Coleman mentioned that the woman who had worked there before me had gone to work at Vanderbilt but she had agreed to come back and train me to do the automated DNA sequencing. I mentioned to Dr. Coleman that I had recently gone back to school and was working on my Master's degree and had classes twice a week that started at 4:40. I asked him if it would be a problem for me to leave a little earlier on those days and he said it was not a problem. This is going to work out I thought to myself. I'm finally making a decent salary and I can keep going to school.

The woman who had been the lab coordinator of the Core Facility was very nice, her name was Eila and she was Indian. No one else at Meharry knew how to do the automated DNA sequencing so she had come back to train me. She said her husband was still a principal investigator there in the Microbiology Department. Eila explained that she loved her job there and did not want to leave, but she needed to transfer over to Vanderbilt for the tuition benefit. She had two sons and she wanted to be able to send them to college. By the time we had finished the training she shared that her husband had lost their savings on the Stock Market day trading. I sympathized with her situation and the sacrifice that she was making for her children. I had also lost money myself trying to trade stocks online just as the bubble was bursting.

Chapter Thirteen

Making the Adjustment

Juggling our day to day schedule turned out to be no joke. I had to take my lunch to work every day because I worked straight through, picked up Casey at 3:00 on the days that Cornelius couldn't make it, picked up Kim after band practice or swim practice depending on what day it was, and went back to work or to class depending on what day it was. It was rough, but I wouldn't have changed a thing. I was able to make my classes without any conflict with the kid's afterschool activities and that was important to me.

The semester was going quickly and there was a lot more work with three classes than one. I used the weekends to catch up on my reading and assignments. The office that I made for myself in the extra bedroom when we built our house was really serving its purpose. I have to say my new job was a Godsend, there was a relaxed atmosphere and the students were always refreshing to talk with. Sometimes they needed advice or encouragement and that was something that I had learned a lot about. I had been encouraging myself for almost five years. I was also able to find time between my responsibilities to do some research on the group project and design our survey for the health fair at the YMCA.

There were two men in the group who turned out to be useless. What usually happens with men in mixed group settings is that they either take over everything or do absolutely nothing and leave most of the work on the women. I thought we should divide the presentation and the paper into four parts, but it turned out to be a bad idea when one whole section was missing. My decision not to do more than my share on the class presentation of our project and on the paper left us with a mediocre grade as a group. When the semester ended in the first week of May, I was happy for a short break. I had made two 'A's in the Leadership and Education Law classes, but I had gotten a 'B' on the Education Research class. If I could go back and do it differently I would. I learned that if you want to be excellent sometimes you have to carry other people even if you don't think it's fair. In a group, either you take them with you or they hold you back.

***

Between the semesters I decided to go and see an arthritis specialist. I found Dr. Girard's office when I was driving back from the kids dance classes on Charlotte Ave. Sitting at the red light I saw a sign that said rheumatoid arthritis specialist. During my appointment he explained that there was a laundry list of drugs available to treat rheumatoid arthritis and that we would take our time to find the one that best suited me. He said that once we found the right one I would not feel any stiffness or pain. Dr. Girard recommended that we begin with prednisone, a steroid that would relieve my inflammation, and then we would move up the ladder until my joints became more comfortable. Our objective was to keep inflammation down to prevent permanent joint damage. I had heard of prednisone before, my aunt Cassy had taken it after her kidney transplant and I knew it was something given to cancer patients to increase their appetite. I really wasn't happy about taking it with all the side effects, but I need to get some relief for my knees. I started taking two tablets before bed and after a while I could feel some improvement.

The girls would be out of school for the summer soon and

that would slow down our pace some which would make it the best time for me to take classes. I discovered there were some free summer programs on the TSU campus that the girls could participate in. They were academic enrichment programs and would give me a break from paying the cost of the Fisk mini-college program since I had more tuition to pay. The girls were not happy about it but they would survive. I planned to take three more classes and two internships for a total of eleven hours during the summer and with the escalated schedule I would have to work my buns off to get it done.

I was taking School Finance, Socio/Political Issues for Schools, and I had Dr. Hullette again for the Planning for an Educational Facility class. It was going to be a feat to pull off, but I couldn't afford not to succeed at these prices. The internships would have to be the shadowing of a Principal or a top administrator at an educational facility. The difficulties were finding a principal during summer school who would allow me to shadow them and leaving work early four days a week to pick up the girls get them home and get to class by 4:40 on Monday and Wednesday and 5:00 on Tuesday and Thursday.

There were only two school sites where there would be summer school classes for high school students, Stratford in East Nashville and Hillsboro in South Nashville. Hillsboro was closer to my job so I called and made an appointment with the principal. Kim had just finished her freshman year at Hillsboro so I was familiar with the school. I was anxious about the meeting because I couldn't take no for an answer, I didn't have any other options.

Mr. Johnson came into the outer office and shook my hand. He was a congenial man, tall and slender with graying hair and wire framed glasses. He welcomed me into his office and offered me a seat. I explained to him that my daughter was a student at Hillsboro and that I was working on my Master's degree and needed to do an administrative internship. I went on to show him the requirements for the internship, the number of hours required, and the duties that I should experience during the summer semester.

"That sounds like something that I'd be happy to do for the parent of one of our Hillsboro students," he said to me.

He probably knew that he had made my day.

Mr. Johnson took me on a tour of the school grounds while we continued to talk. He talked about how the students who attended Hillsboro Summer School would be from schools all over the city. He explained the many reasons why some would be attending. Some had missed too many days to pass, others refused to do any class work, and others wanted to get ahead in the next school year. We walked further and he showed me some of the maintenance problems of the school. Things that were old and needed to be replaced and things they had patched together.

On the way back to his office he told me that he was originally from Arizona and hoped to return there in the near future. He showed me his pedometer and said that he had recently had a heart attack and had been diagnosed with diabetes. He told me how that motivated him to change his whole diet and lifestyle and from that he had lost fifty pounds. That was impressive. Checking his pedometer he told me that he tried to take 10,000 steps per day. When we returned to his office, we made a schedule of 8:00 to 10:00 every day for three weeks to get thirty hours. I thanked him for his time and the opportunity to shadow him and rushed back to work.

My days consisted of getting the kids to their summer program, going by the job to open up the Core facility, then driving across town to Hillsboro for my internship and then going back to work until around 4:00 when I left to pick up the kids and then back to TSU for my evening class. I was running from 6:00 in the morning to 10:00 at night every day.

Shadowing Dr. Johnson, I tried to be there by 8:00 in the

morning when the school day began. We greeted the students at the door as they arrived and he checked for standard school attire and any obvious contraband. He knew most of them by name as he hurried those students who meandered slowly through the hallways into their assigned classrooms. He followed that ritual with a staff meeting on the objectives for the day and any pressing problems from the previous day. He would divide and delegate the responsibilities of the office and then after that he took meetings with those waiting to see him.

One was with a white father and son; the son had an individual education program (IEP) that said he couldn't write, so he was using that as the reason why his assignments had not been done. Dr. Johnson suggested that he use a tape recorder to tape whatever he couldn't write to the dismay of both father and son who wanted him excused from the assignments. Another meeting was with a Hispanic student sent to the office for sleeping in class. Right away Dr. Johnson asked him how many hours he was working at night and he said ten. I was stunned, that was a lot for a teenager. Dr. Johnson told him to try and get his hours cut down for the next three weeks until the first summer session was done.

Over the week he handled fights between students, fights between students and teachers, teachers who were missing too many days, and believe it or not teachers who were improperly dressed. We would take time to talk about each situation, he would tell me why he chose his reaction, and he would ask me what I would do in the same instance. He used every opportunity to teach me something and I was learning how involved his job was. I would usually dash back to work after our conferences trying to skim off as many minutes before 10:00 as I could.

I had to make sure that I kept all my bases covered at work. Dr. Coleman was allowing me so much flexibility, coming in late and leaving early, that I did not want to fall short in any way. There was no pressure or stress in the environment and I wanted to do everything that I could to keep it that way. The students were calling me Miss Karen and it surprised me at first and made me feel older. Cornelius said it was out of respect, but to me it was respect for an elder. We laughed and he said that the younger guys on his job were calling him 'Old School' and he reminded them that he had been in his twenties at one time too. I was thankful that I was finally in a place where I was appreciated as a worker and allowed some professional courtesies.

***

Some days when I got to class it was the first time that I had a chance to sit down for more than five minutes. I would spend the first thirty minutes of the class settling down and catching my breath. Most of the students complained that the classes were too long, but I needed that much time to sit and relax. I got a kick out of the socio/political issues of education class where we discussed solutions that would create incentives for children to excel in school. We looked at examples of some schools where the concept of paying students money was having a positive impact on achievement.

The School Finance class was an eye opener for me, it explained how budgets were designed and that mysterious per pupil dollar amount and how they arrived at the number. Yet again, it was Dr. Hullette's class that taught the planning for an educational facility that worked my butt off. He took us out for tours in all the buildings on campus pointing out small details and the purposes for them. He got trial memberships for all of us to use this software that allowed us to design our own classroom on the computer. He even had each of us to go to one of the metro schools and do an evaluation of the facility.

One night after my school finance class ended, I tried to stand up and my legs wouldn't move. It was crazy to me. They hadn't been aching or bothering me in any way during class. It's was as if they were locked in the sitting position. I began to get panicky as I remembered Dr. Girard saying that all of a sudden some people are not able to walk with severe rheumatoid arthritis. I pretended to be busy organizing my things as the rest of the class filtered out of the door. When I was alone in the room I tried to force my legs to straighten out and stand. I tried massaging the joints to loosen them, but when I tried to put weight on them it felt like sharp knives were cutting into my bones. I felt so stupid, why didn't I ask someone to help me before everyone left.

It was my own feelings of embarrassment or wanting to appear younger that had me there alone and unable to move. I just stood there in the class by my desk for a few minutes hoping to wake up my legs. I picked up my books and purse and then took a step. Each step was agonizing as I made it out of the door and into the hallway. I would have to stop and wait after taking a few steps because the pain was unbearable as the knives kept jabbing me in the legs. Outside of the building I knew I would never make it down the stairs, so I just took baby steps down the long handicapped ramp.

It was scary, this side of the campus seemed deserted. Finally after I got down the handicap ramp I still had a long distance between me and my car. I saw the campus police phone and was tempted to call and ask for help or an ambulance, but it was my crazy vanity that made me keep walking by the phone. A male student walked across the walkway headed to another building ahead of me. He looked my way and I gave him a small smile as if everything was okay. I thought for a minute that if someone came to do harm to me I couldn't have run two steps for my life. I almost laughed as the scene ran through my mind. I didn't have my phone, besides Cornelius was at work and who else could I call. I just prayed, "Help me Lord," as I took one painful step at a time. It seemed like it took forever but I eventually made it to the parking lot and into my car.

I drove home in silence, turning the radio off, not wanting to hear the noise, my brain was in overload. It seemed like whenever things got on track the other shoe would drop. I wanted to just break down and cry but the kids would notice my swollen face and red eyes and I didn't want them to worry about me. I started praying again, knowing that the Lord Jesus had not brought me this far to leave me. I remembered my prayer, "Great is thy faithfulness O Lord, from the rising of the sun to the going down of the same, Your name is worthy to be praised."

When I got home and went to step out of the car most of the pain in my legs was gone and I could walk up the stairs. Kim and Casey ran to meet me at the door, they had begun to worry because I had come home later than they had expected. I could tell they were relieved to see me and I was glad to be home. I think all of us were super sensitive about each other and worried when one of us was out of sight. There had been many nights I laid awake until I heard the garage door open and saw Cornelius come in the door.

When Cornelius got home that night I told him what had happened and he wanted me to call the doctor first thing in the morning. My legs were stiff when I woke up but not much different than they usually were so I decided to call Dr. Girard after I finished shadowing Mr. Johnson at Hillsboro.

Mr. Johnson and I had a very serious conversation the next morning about the state of education among poor people in America. He told me we were fighting a losing battle and that most of the kids didn't even want to be here. His usual upbeat attitude was missing and I thought he was just having a bad day, having seen too much over his many years of teaching and administrating and was feeling burned out. I began to think about my interest in teaching as we did our morning round of looking in on a few classrooms. I was beginning to see that I had a romanticized idea of what it was like to teach. It wasn't like the TV shows or the movies represented. It was hard work that didn't always have a happy ending. It was against the resistance of the students, and in some cases even hindered by the parents.

I had been infected by Mr. Johnson's melancholy mood that morning and I carried it back with me to work.

I was less worried about my legs after my phone call to Dr. Girard, he said that the episode that I had experienced can happen with rheumatoid arthritis and I should never sit for more than thirty minutes at a time without standing up and moving around. He also mentioned that I shouldn't stay on the steroids too long and that we would begin to talk about trying the next medication on the list when I came for my next visit. That incident was enough for me to closely monitor how long I was in a seated position. I began to realize how much time I spent sitting with all the reading and writing assignments.

At work I would take my books over to the lab bench and read standing up where I could keep my joints moving. My schedule didn't leave me much time for walking or even getting on the treadmill, and by the time I got home around 9:00 I was toasted. I would try to spend a little time with Kim and Casey before they went to bed. I began to make an effort to walk through the neighborhood around Meharry at least three times a week when I had the time. My schedule was a killer but it was bringing me back to life.

The graduate students at work gave me an added extra benefit at work, I felt a kinship with them and I became close to several of them. The struggle of living life while going to school has its special challenges that I knew very well. They would come to me for advice and I knew what they needed, it's what we all need, encouragement to stay in the game. Someone to help us see the finish line, someone to help us believe we can make it, and someone who can point out the path of least resistance. I tried to help them learn what I had learned, that it wasn't going to be easy and there was no shortage of obstacles. We don't have a choice if we want to succeed, we have to keep pushing forward, and quitting is not an option.

I was also learning that I had more of a connection with undergraduate and graduate students than with high school students. Teaching younger students is a true calling, so many of our youth lack the motivation to learn, throw that in with a short attention span, and it takes a special person to be able to educate in that environment. I was learning in my socio/political education class that the key to increasing academic achievement was in creating incentives for students especially low-income students to learn. To me it was relatively simple, they respond to the incentives that every other red-blooded American citizen responds to, money. Nevertheless, the powers that be, or better known as the wealthy, don't want the poor to be corrupted by money. They tell us we should do things because of noble reasons and because it's the right thing to do to make us better people. So much for leading by example.

***

The summer months are always the fastest ones, my second internship with Mr. Johnson was wrapping up and he discussed his plans for him and his wife to retire and move back to Arizona. He made me think about wanting to do something that would fulfill me in a career not leave me feeling empty. I was seriously questioning if teaching was really what I wanted to do. I planned to talk about it after class with Dr. Hullette, he always seemed to have this great insight on a variety of subjects and he had changed careers many times and I admired the courage and tenacity he had to do that. I wanted to do that.

My conversation with Dr. Hullette cleared my mind, he explained to me that I had been continuously working in higher education since college and that's where I should stay.

"Why start all over again in something you don't know anything about when you have experience in higher education," Dr. Hullette said. "Build on what you have. There are many areas in higher education that would interest you. There is also the option of getting your doctorate and teaching on the university level."

"I never thought I could do something like that," I answered.

"Well think about it," he said.

I definitely intended to.

Our summer vacation approached around the end of the semester. I had learned a lot from my calculus class last summer, and I started writing the required papers for the classes as soon as I got my syllabus. All of my papers were written and waiting to be handed in.

The summer school session for metro was also drawing to a close. On the last day of my internship Mr. Johnson and I took our customary walk around the school grounds. He had been so kind and gracious to me and I expressed to him how much that meant to me. He had given me an inside view into the teaching profession as a teacher and as an administrator. Mr. Johnson had shown me the power that the school board has in influencing the education of public school students. I honestly couldn't see myself starting a new career as a teacher for high school students as I had before this experience. The bureaucracy within the school system kept many from truly making a difference. Fortunately I had the security of a job that would allow me the time to find out where I was supposed to be.

Chapter Fourteen

New Horizons

For this year's vacation to travel somewhere we had never been, we were going to cruise to the Virgin Islands. St. Thomas and St. Maarten were two of the most beautiful places I had ever seen. The jewel colors of the water are indescribable. It was the perfect blend of the magnificent with the simplistic that gave both cities their distinct flavor. In St. Thomas you could see a goat standing in the front yard beside a Mercedes car, and a stately home with laundry hanging out to dry on the line. In St. Maarten, a walk downtown looks like that of any east coast city complete with vendors selling incense, jewelry and bootleg CD's, and then turn down an alley and find one of the most spectacular views of the ocean on God's earth.

The people were kind and more laid back than those in Haiti or Jamaica. Of all the places I have had a chance to visit, these I would love to come back to see over and over again. I thanked the Lord for blessing me with the opportunity to see the beauty of his world. Sometimes when we go through tragedies or hardships it feels like the Lord has forsaken us and turned His back on us. It's only when we come through that storm that we realize He blessed us through it. It is hard to accept that His will is not always our will, but He has always kept his promises and been an ever present help and source of strength through our times of trouble.

"I praise You for Your steadfast love that never ceases, for it is renewed every morning. Great is Your faithfulness, O Lord."

We were welcomed back into the whirlwind when we got back to Nashville, the other high cost of taking time off. I had two finals to take and papers to turn in. Things had stacked up at work while I was gone, and it was time to get Kim and Casey ready for a new school year. Kim's fifteenth birthday was also coming up but I was ready for it and I was feeling relieved, she had made it through the fourteenth year. I had kept my anxieties to myself as usual so no one knew what it meant to me.

I waited a week after the semester ended before I went to the myTSU website to check my grades. I was so happy, I had made four 'A's and a 'B' in my second internship. I was greedy now, I wanted all 'A's but I hadn't really made all the hours that were required. I didn't complain, it was hard and stressful trying to run between my job and Hillsboro High School in the mornings, trying to determine which was my first priority, but with Dr. Coleman's indulgence I had juggled them both as well as I could.

I went into the fall semester with great expectations. I only lacked ten hours from completing my Master's degree. I went to my departmental advisor and discussed what classes were needed just to be sure and then I registered for them.

The advanced educational psychology was an eye opening class for me. The chapter on self-efficacy explained why so many of us limit ourselves and fall short of our potential. Our self-efficacy is our belief system about ourselves and our abilities. I discovered that I, like many of us, had an inner belief that certain achievements were out of my range, not consciously, but subconsciously. I dreamed small and set goals for myself that I thought were attainable without really thinking about it. I thought about the many things that I now believed I was probably capable of doing and the list is much longer than it was when I was younger. Ironically, now I'm not sure if I have the time to fulfill them.

It was a tough semester, none of my classes were offered on the weekend, so I was in class until around 9:00 two days a week and until 10:00 at least once a week. Kim was in marching band so she had band practice after school for two days, she also had swim practice with the Hillsboro swim team, and the band played on Fridays at the football games and traveled with the Hillsboro Football team for away games. We had to break down and get Kim a cell phone so we could keep up with the schedules and the unforeseen changes. I spent a good amount of time behind the wheel trying to get us all where we needed to be.

There were a couple of times when Kim was at some practice and Casey didn't have her dance class that I didn't have anyone to watch her and she had to ride on the bus with Cornelius until I got out of class. Casey was still pretty young, only seven in the 2nd grade, and there were times I felt guilty that I wasn't giving her the time that I had given the other girls, but I also knew that I was a better person and a better mother since I had gone back to school. It wasn't perfect, sometimes I thought we worked well as a team and other times I felt we were drifting apart in different directions, but everybody seemed well adjusted and content.

An additional requirement for graduation was the passing of the comprehensive exam which included questions from every class in the curriculum. All the students had been warned not to take the exam until you are ready because you were only allowed to take it twice and it was not uncommon for quite a few to fail it. All the questions are essay and the exam is graded by at least three professors to give a fair judgment of the answers. I began preparing a notebook that I would use to study between the reading and writing assignments. I didn't want to get in the stressful position of trying to cram a large amount of information into my head in a short amount of time. I didn't just want to memorize facts I wanted to digest the knowledge.

With most of my time consumed with working and going to school every day the house was never as clean as I used to keep it and dust balls were gathering behind the doors. There were days when I felt guilty about it but we were all busy and tired so we just got by with the basics, basic cleaning, basic meals, and basic time together. Despite all that was going on, halfway through the semester I felt positive enough to tell people I was going to graduate in December.

My brother in California, Dell, threw a bucket of cold water on my news when I told him.

"Is it from a real school?" he asked.

What was that supposed to mean, why would he asked that? I guess he thought maybe I had been going to a half-baked on-line college. It goes to show that while you may have low expectations for yourself, there's always someone who has even lower expectations for you. I let that water roll right off my back and shared the news with my sister, Helene, in Philadelphia. She was so happy for me that she said she wouldn't miss it and that she was coming to see me graduate. I knew that her money was funny and she probably wouldn't be able to come but it made me feel great. I also called my Aunt Lilly and she said she was so proud of me. She had an idea of where I had been and what it took to get to this point.

The comprehensive exam was scheduled for the Saturday after TSU Homecoming and I was nervous about what questions would be asked. Whenever I would ask someone who had taken it for clues about the test they would give vague answers accompanied by memory lapses. I guess they weren't going to give an advantage to someone else that they didn't have and I could understand that. All's fair in love and war and preparing for an exam.

The test was given in two parts. We took the first part of the essay in the morning and the second part after lunch. It was so stressful that everyone went their separate ways for lunch not even wanting to talk. We all wanted to use the extra time to review before the second half. I sat out in the car eating the lunch I had packed for myself while I studied my notes. Essay questions are tricky, sometimes it's hard to know the answer that the professor is looking for and the exam was either a pass or a fail. My strategy was to answer each question from different perspectives.

After the exam I drove home and went straight to bed, I felt like I had run in a marathon. Now all I had to do was get my research paper written and I could cross the finish line. It was around two weeks later that I got a letter in the mail that said that I had passed my comprehensive exam. It was official then, I was going to get my Master's degree.

Dr. Hullette and I had a conversation after class on the last day. I told him I had considered the things he said and that he was right. I had decided to keep my emphasis in higher education.

"Are you going to enter the doctorate program?" he asked.

"I hope to," I answered, even though I had not seriously thought about it.

Several students in my classes had talked about it and I had toyed with the idea in my head, but it wasn't something that I had ever planned on doing. Discussing it out loud gave it weight and substance and it became real to me. If other students who struggled with the master's program could do it, why couldn't I? I asked around and learned that you could register for nine hours before you were admitted into the program. That would give me enough time to submit my resume, write an essay, and get the four recommendation letters required with the application for admission. I finished out the semester with 'A's in all my classes and was more confident that I should keep moving this thing further.

The process for graduation was similar for the graduate school, but this time I felt more excitement as I picked up my cap and gown and the hood for distinction. I had more of a sense of accomplishment than I had last year and I wanted to celebrate my hard work. Helene made the trip to Nashville as she had promised just to see me graduate and I was overwhelmed that she thought it was important enough to come. I was so happy to be at this point that I decided to throw myself a party after graduation.

At the commencement rehearsal Dr. Lockheed was in his

usual position as taskmaster overseeing the process, providing the graduates with his usual marching orders and threats. When I received my number and we lined up I could see that my status had changed. Graduate degree candidates marched ahead of the undergraduate class and that made it even more special. I couldn't wait to walk across that stage again.

Same as the year before, Cornelius dropped me off first and returned later with my mother, sister, and the girls. None of my other relatives were going to be there and I thought about human nature and how people are more willing to share a sorrowful occasion with you than a joyful one. Standing in the hallway among the other graduates I saw a few classmates and we stepped out of line and hugged and congratulated each other. Waiting for that magic time when the music started I was so proud of myself. It felt good to be wearing the hood for the Master's degree, the distinction that told everybody there that you had taken it to the next level.

Walking out to that familiar music my heart was so full with gratefulness. I had been given a new life. I had a right to it, I had earned it. After all the graduates had entered the room the audience began to applaud and I knew a part of the recognition was for me. As the ceremony proceeded on I just wanted to absorb the moment and keep it forever. Simply sitting in my chair among a floor full of graduates was one of the most exhilarating experiences of my life as my mind traveled back over the years.

No one around me had known what I had gone through and how far I had come to be sitting there, they didn't know it was a miracle that I was seated in that chair, and it didn't matter. I knew my story, my journey, and I was overcome with gratitude for the Lord Jesus delivering me through it all, hearing my heartfelt and desperate plea as I walked those 72 steps up that hill. He had answered me, he had strengthened and restored me, and I was truly born again. I was changed, not because of a degree, but in my mind and heart, in my whole being and my perception of who I was. I was valuable and worthy. I was a survivor, a great lady, bad to the bone. I had been knocked down and counted out, but the Lord had mercy on me and He picked me up. And for every step I took He carried me two. I was so thankful. I knew that I could do anything and I wanted to keep growing. It took all I had to keep from shouting but I held my blind mule back lest Dr. Lockheed have me carried out of there with a police escort. If only I could have bottled that feeling, I'd be a millionaire.

Cornelius gave me a beautiful sapphire necklace as a graduation gift when I got home and I was blown away, I hadn't expected anything. The after party was anticlimactic, even though my sister had flown a long distance none of my relatives in the city showed up, a few neighbors and my pastor came, and we had more food than we knew what to do with, but nothing could steal the elation of the day and what it meant to me personally. I was inspired by what God had done in my life, and I knew it wasn't over. I wanted to do some of the things that Courtney did not have the time to do. I wanted her to continue to live through me, so I had to live to my life's fullest. It was on. I was going for the doctorate. It would be more challenging than the master's with 60 hours required; twice the number of class hours for the master's degree, but I was committed. My father always wanted one of his children to be a doctor, why couldn't it be me?

Chapter Fifteen

New Challenges

I thought about all the potential that is lost in the world and it spurred me on to try and achieve as much as I could personally. One of my concerns after the holidays was if we could afford for me to continue to use the credit cards to pay for my tuition. Cornelius and I talked about it, and decided that if I was going to do this I should take out a student loan. That was a hard decision to make, being that it had taken me fifteen years to pay back fourteen thousand from my undergraduate years, but with the high interest on credit cards and the pace that I was charging tuition I would never be able to pay them off. So my new friend's name was Sallie Mae, the student loan service center for graduate students after taking out a loan for $10,000.

The New Year, 2007, was the beginning of my new venture. I kept quiet about my studies, it wasn't as if there was much interest in my last project, and I didn't want to answer a ton of questions about what I was doing or why. I didn't understand it myself, it was a path that the Lord was laying out for me and I didn't know where it would lead. I registered for nine hours in the spring semester and things were going well. I found that most of the students in the doctoral program were closer to my age and a lot were older than I was, some looked as if they had already retired, and that definitely made me feel more like a real college student again.

The cold and wet winter weather was causing me some serious inflammation flare-ups in my knees that made them swell and it was painful to walk at times. Dr. Girard recommended we try some other medications and changed my prescription, but the different medication was wrecking havoc on my digestive system. My stomach would bloat with gas and make noises regardless of what I ate. It had become embarrassing sitting in class with my stomach talking out loud during quiet exams as if I held a microphone to my tummy. I found that if I held it in as tight as I could it would contain a lot of the noise but that took great effort after a few minutes. I tried another medication that was basically an antibiotic, but it only made me feel worse. I finally gave in and started taking the methotrexate and I was pleased, to say the least, that my hair didn't fall out and I didn't have the other awful side effects.

    The schedule around the house hadn't changed much and I was still driving criss-cross through the city to get from work to the kids and back to school. One day I was driving to pick Kim up from swim practice at the Glencliff pool and a light rain was causing problems on the interstate. The traffic was heavy as rush hour began and impatient drivers would speed up only to have to stop within a few yards. The drive was tedious with quick starts and short stops.

    My mind wandered as I sat during one of the stops going over a long to-do list until I felt a tremendous jolt to the car that hurled me forward and jerked me back. I looked in the rearview mirror and saw a small truck had crashed into the back of me, and I had bumped into the car in front of me. At first I didn't realize that I had been in a serious car accident, I just thought that I was going to be late to pick up Kim and late to class, but after I got out and looked at the damage I knew it had to be reported. I called the police and got back in the car, disgusted that the guy who caused the accident didn't even get out of his truck to check if I was alright. The man in the car in front of me who I bumped came back and asked me if I needed an ambulance and I told him that I didn't. He mentioned that he called the police also. I called Cornelius and told him that I had gotten hit on the interstate but I was fine. He said that he would call in to work, pick up Kim and they would try to get over to where I was as soon as he could.

It wasn't long before a policeman got there and made his report and left after I told him I didn't need a tow. I called Kim and Cornelius on the phone and told them I was kind of nervous sitting in the inside lane and that I was going to drive the car home and see them there. Traffic was heavy all over town because of the rain so they agreed. When I got home they were waiting outside and when Kim saw how bad the car was damaged her eyes filled with tears. I guess it was disconcerting to look at the car and know I could have been hurt.

Cornelius thought that I should go to emergency to get checked out and I thought it might be a good suggestion. My neck was starting to stiffen up and was I wondering if the rheumatoid arthritis might complicate an injury. Cornelius drove me to Centennial Emergency, which wasn't crowded, and I had a short wait before I saw a doctor.

The attending physician was a black guy who explained that you don't actually feel the effects of a car accident right away, that people usually wake up sore the next day. He asked me to do a few movements which I couldn't and by the time we were finished he told me I had suffered minor whiplash in the accident but other than that I was fine. I was thankful for that and just wanted to go home and sleep, it had been a long day. He said I didn't need a neck brace and wrote me prescriptions for pain and muscle relaxers.

I called in sick the next day when I woke up; I was still achy, sore, and tired. Nevertheless, I couldn't afford to miss class, two days missed and you lost a letter grade, so Cornelius left me his truck to get to class.

The next night I woke up with a piercing pain in my leg. As the minutes went by I became more alarmed as my imagination ran away with me. What if it was a blood clot, what if it moved to my heart or my lungs? I just kept laying there in fear, in pain, and in silence until I couldn't take it anymore.

I woke up Cornelius and told him my leg was throbbing.
"Is it in the joint?" he asked.
"No," I said, "It's shooting all the way down my leg."
He suggested that I take some of the pain pills I was prescribed from the accident. After about thirty minutes I got some relief, they didn't take away all the pain, but it was enough for me to calm down and wait until the morning. I called Dr. Sanders our primary physician and he told me to come on in. After he examined me he said it was probably the sciatic nerve that had been aggravated by being rear-ended. He said that I would need to start physical therapy for that and for my neck injury. The physical therapy clinic was located on the same floor so he sent me right over to be evaluated. The therapist, Eve, was very nice and gentle. The only drawback was that she wanted me to come to her office two or three times a week. I told her it would be easier to make it just twice a week and I would do the exercises she gave me at home, so she agreed.

The next day at work I told Dr. Coleman that I would have to start physical therapy as a result of the accident. These are the days that I am grateful that he is a man of few words. I was already running in and out picking up my kids and leaving early to go to class, now add physical therapy appointments. My boss was such a blessing to me and I made sure I gave my best on the job in thanks for all of his understanding.

Over the next few days I learned a lot about car insurance. The insurance company of the truck that hit me determined that my car was totaled because the amount to fix it was more than the car was worth according to the Blue Book. They had decided not to fix it and give me what it was worth at the time which they said was between $2800 and $3200 and that I had to surrender my car to them. I explained to the adjustor that I needed to get my car fixed and I needed to keep it, to which she said they would only give me the salvage price of $1200. That was not going to work, I knew that I was driving around in a ten year old car, but it was paid for. I couldn't take on a car note while I was trying to go to school; tuition and books were more than we could stand. Fortunately my insurance company opted to fix my car and go after the other insurance company for reimbursement.

Then came the onslaught of ambulance chasers and chiropractors calling me morning, noon, and night. I hadn't had this many strangers wanting to work to help me in my entire life. So many lawyers from so many firms had been advising me to protect myself from future complications and offered horror stories about people who didn't realize they had suffered serious long-term injuries and were later disabled. That did make me think about arthritis jumping in my neck and back and so I consulted with Bart Durham when his firm called because I recognized him from the TV commercials.

I remembered when Cornelius and I consulted with a medical malpractice attorney on behalf of Courtney and he told us that it would be hard to prove our case since doctors rarely went against one another. Now I was barely hurt and I couldn't get past the pack of lawyers wanting to make sure my medical bills were covered and I received money for pain and suffering. After a while I realized that they just wanted me to run up a heap of doctor's bills so they could maximize their portion of a settlement. I decided that I wasn't going to suffer through treatments for their benefit. It wasn't worth the trouble for me.

***

The classes were smaller in the doctoral program than in the master's, which meant there was much more participation from students in classroom discussions. In most of the classes we actually set around a conference table together. I was learning quite a bit and starting to feel like a real intellectual. The writing and research assignments were constant and with three classes I squeezed in computer research and writing at work and at home whenever I could.

I hoped that seeing me work hard in my classes would help motivate Kim because it was time for her to prepare to go to college. I encouraged her to keep her grades up so she would have a good chance at getting an academic scholarship.

"Higher education doesn't come cheap and it never goes on sale," I said, "Your parents aren't rich."

I didn't think she wasn't convinced, but there was a program called Avid at Hillsboro that helped encouraged high school students to prepare for college. When I got a call asking if she could participate I couldn't say yes fast enough.

The spring flew by with me doing my thing and when the semester and school year ended we were all ready for a break. Southwest had a special on flights to Oakland, California so we took the opportunity to fly out and visit my brother in a city I had never been before. I had never traveled further west than Las Vegas so it was good to finally see the west coast. We crossed the Bay Bridge and toured San Francisco and saw the sites that I had heard about and seen on television. The city couldn't meet the high expectations that I had built over a lifetime, but it was fun to ride the street car I had seen so many times in the commercial for "Rice-a-Roni that San Francisco treat" and shop in China town.

I think that after seeing the beauty of the Caribbean, the brown waters around San Francisco couldn't compete. I had heard that once you visit there you want to live there, but I didn't feel that way. I began to realize that we sometimes romanticize the lives of family and friends and that we all lead a similar existence, the variation is in the personal relationships that we have and the value we place on them. There is nothing fulfilling about a place by itself, it's the experiences that we share with people there that make the difference.

When we got back to Nashville, Kim started taking an ACT preparation course for the summer, Casey was enrolled at an academic enrichment program at Shrader Lane Church, and I registered for the summer session. I discovered that registering for twelve hours cost the same amount of tuition as registering for nine hours, so when you're paying cash you have to maximize your money. I registered for twelve hours. I hadn't taken four full classes before, not including the internships and I was definitely overloaded. If I hadn't known the amount of effort required for working on a doctorate before now, I did learn that semester.

The terminal degree was about research and becoming an expert or authority on the subject of your research. As candidates we were told our objective was to further build on the body of knowledge from our chosen subject or focus. I was taking two classes that were the backbone of the doctoral program, Advance Methods for Research and Statistical Analysis. It was at this point that candidates should know what the subject for their research should be.

Dr. Hullette was the professor in my Advance Methods for Research class and he grilled us one by one in class on our areas of interests to assist us in narrowing down to a topic for our dissertation. He didn't pull any punches and told a few their choices for research were unacceptable. He also told a few people that he didn't know how they got here, that they were wasting their time, and didn't belong in the doctoral program. For the rest of us he stressed the importance on choosing a topic that was relevant and not overdone. He also described the pitfalls that had befallen some students, leaving them ABD, which meant "all but dissertation" and that was the place that none of us wanted to end up.

When I was working on the master's degree I became interested in the policies that increase or decrease educational opportunities for minorities to go to college. It was a subject that was dear to my heart and impacted me personally. I decided to focus on the Tennessee Lottery and on how the HOPE scholarships were biased against minorities and the socioeconomically disadvantaged when they were the people who played the lottery at disproportionately higher levels. Any research, reading, and papers that followed were to be centered on the topic for our dissertation.

The four classes were working me like a dog so I was glad to have the evenings free from activities for the kids during the summer. The statistics class gave me the most trouble. Dr. Nelson was the instructor and he had just gotten the news that he had received a prestigious fellowship to teach in India. From our lectures, I thought his body was here but his mind had already left for the East. We were given software and taught how to build study sets and run the analysis, but how to relate that information to our projects was a bit shaky. At the end of the semester I had aced three of the classes, but I got a C in the statistical analysis class. No 'C's are allowed in graduate school it was like and 'F'. The class had to be repeated. It hurt my feelings as well as my pocketbook. I didn't feel I deserved a 'C', but Dr. Nelson had left the country by the time grades came out and there was nothing I could do about it.

***

Our summer vacation came right on time, we all needed a break. My sister Helene and her daughter Brianna were traveling with us on a cruise to Canada. It was something that we had talked about doing, but money was always scarce. We spent the evening in Atlantic City walking up and down the Boardwalk with the kids before driving up to get on the Carnival ship in New York the next morning. It was different sailing out of New York versus Florida. It was misty on the water and I thought about the movies I had seen about immigrants coming to America when we sailed past the Statue of Liberty.

The girls enjoyed the extra company and we had a good time together. Kim and Brianna were on the karaoke stage every night singing and dancing. I was a little concerned about Helene though, she didn't look like herself. Her face seemed drawn and contorted as if she were in pain or some kind of distress. When we were leaving the ship in St. John I asked her if she and Brianna wanted to wait on the ship and rest, but they wanted us to stay together and go out on the excursion with us. I felt nervous and guilty the whole time. I felt like I was pushing her to walk further and faster than she was comfortable with but she never complained and she didn't want to stop and rest. We had a great time on the trip, but I believe we were all more tired on the way home than we were when we started out to get some rest and relaxation. We had a long drive from New York to Philly and then to Nashville, but it was a great ending to the busy summer.

Chapter Sixteen

Help Us Lord

In the Fall I took another twelve hours that included repeating the statistical analysis class, there was no way around it, so why put it off. Things were more hectic with school back in and Kim had added another after school activity, half-time dancer. It conflicted with her swim schedule at the Nashville Aquatic Club and she said she didn't care, she wanted to dance. She decided she would just swim for the Hillsboro swim team so she could practice with the half-timers. It bothered me because the girl was a natural born swimmer. The water loved her and from the point of view of someone who sinks like a rock she didn't know it was a gift. So I let go of my dreams of her going to the Olympics and gave her my blessing. The child could dance her butt off and I wanted the girls to take advantage of every opportunity to express themselves and use their talents and find their passion in life. Hectic was our new normal so we just rolled on.

My sister Helene was having some more health problems and whenever we talked on the phone she spoke of hitting the wall on her job and how much it stressed her out. She said she had no energy and was feeling so bad that she had been home sick for three weeks. Helene and I were always close. Whenever I didn't feel like Kim was treating Casey like she should I would tell her how my sister Helene treated me when we were younger.

She wasn't just a sister, she was a big sister. Someone I looked up to and someone who had always looked out for me. I remember her fighting a boy in the street to protect me when I was young, and her sneaking into the kitchen in the middle of the night to get me something to eat when I woke up hungry. We shared a room all the years we grew up and she comforted me whenever I got into trouble. We have been confidants all our lives, and I knew she had my back even more than Cornelius did.

Helene called me one day around the beginning of September to tell me she was in the hospital. She had been exhausted for several weeks, could hardly walk without falling, and had put on a lot of fluid weight. At first she thought that maybe her blood sugar was high and her kidneys were stressed, so she started taking more insulin and some herbal things to give her kidneys a pick me up. Helene said that between 2:00 and 3:00 in the morning she felt horrible and she could barely breathe. She called 911, told them the door was open and to come right in, and then called my younger sister, Althea, to tell her she was going to the hospital.

After a few days and the loss of fifty pounds of fluid, the doctors at St. Joseph's told her that she had congestive heart failure and they were transferring her to Pennsylvania Hospital. She described how the doctors explained to her that she had come to the hospital just in time, if she would have tried to wait until the morning she probably would not have made it. I was stunned by the whole thing, I thought Helene was invincible. I asked her if I should come up to Philly and she said just wait until she got out of the hospital. We talked more about what made her call 911 that night, and we were both thankful that she did, that she was okay and getting the treatment she needed.

It was less than a week later that my brother Dell called me just as I walked through the door. He said that Helene's heart had stopped and that the doctors were working on her right now. I can't remember much of our conversation after those words but it was very short. I put my books and lunch bag down in the kitchen and walked upstairs to my bedroom. I closed the door and then I laid out prostrate on my bedroom floor and began to pray. I begged the Lord for my sister's life. I didn't want to make the mistake I made when I prayed for Courtney. I pleaded for mercy and grace for my sister.

"Please, Please, oh Lord" I shouted. I wanted the Lord to know I was sincere and not proud. "You are the one in charge, Lord Jesus, not the doctors. Touch my sister's heart, Lord. I'm asking for a miracle, Lord. Let the doctors be in awe of your power, O Lord."

I don't know how long I prayed but I wasn't taking anything for granted. The phone rang again after a while and it was Dell again. I was scared to hear the words as he spoke until he said that Helene was stabilized. He told me how her heart had stopped four times and that the doctors had worked on her for two hours. I leaned against the bed as my legs buckled under me, it was surreal. I could have lost my sister, for some moments I had lost her, but she was back. Dell told me that he was making arrangements to fly into Philadelphia as soon as possible. I told him I was going to get there as soon as I could. A few minutes later I talked to my mother and made arrangements for her to fly up to Philly in a couple of days.

I had so many things to pull together. With my mother out of town and Cornelius's work schedule, I didn't have anyone to get the kids back and forth to school. Talking with Dell after he arrived he told me that Helene was doing better and he let me talk to her on the phone in her room in the ICU. Her voice was scratchy and every response didn't fit what I said but I was glad to hear her voice and she still had her sense of humor.

"I'm not going nowhere," she told me and my heart was lifted.

Dell and I talked some more about what the doctors were saying and he told me to relax that they had things under control. He said the doctors were in awe that when they brought her back after her heart stopping four times in two hours that she didn't have any brain damage. Dell didn't have to say another word after he told me that the doctors were in awe. I almost couldn't contain myself I was so full of joy and thankfulness, because it was then I had my confirmation. I knew that the Lord had heard my prayer and He had answered me and was with my sister. God had not abandoned me and that was good news to me. I shouted and danced and jumped, praising and thanking the Lord Jesus by myself in my own house. God is good all the time, and all the time God is good. Cornelius's Aunt Gladys said she could help with the girls for a few days so I made arrangements to fly up to Philly closer to the weekend.

A few days later before I left town, Dell called me and told me that Helene's heart had stopped again but she was stable again. I was devastated by this setback and I couldn't take being so far away, I had to get there. I brought my prayer book with me, I didn't go anywhere without it, and a CD player to past the time on the plane and in the hospital. On the plane I listened to the Tremaine Hawkins greatest songs CD.

I hadn't been able to listen to the CD since Courtney got sick. It hurt me to hear it because of the memories I had. I used to play it in the car sometimes when I drove the kids around and Courtney and Kim would love to sing "I'm going up yonder" at the top of their lungs when it was on. I tried to listen to it one day several years ago and it broke my heart. I could hear their voices singing along and I couldn't take it. I had taken the CD out of my car and placed it in my nightstand drawer. That morning I saw it as I pulled out my old fashioned CD player and took it with me to Philly.

Dell picked me up from the airport and we drove straight to the hospital. Helene was in the cardiac intensive care unit and as we walked to the area he cautioned me that she was not back to herself yet after the last heart attack. When I got to the room Helene was awake but not aware of us in the room. She was making a guttural sound in a rhythmic way. He said that the brain was in the process of rewiring itself, having been cut off from oxygen for a while. It was disturbing to watch, but she was alive and fighting.

I sat in a chair and read from my prayer book, my mother sang to her, and Dell did tapping across her forehead. Sometimes he would ask us to rub a certain spot on her leg or arm, and I would put my head phones on her ears and play the Tremaine Hawkins CD. The next few days we worked as a team willing her to come back to herself, only leaving her room for meals in the cafeteria. There were times I could really see her fight and struggle and the stress would show on her face. Dell would tap away the tension until she relaxed. Helene improved some each day and was able to talk to us, but my long weekend had flown by and it was time for me to get back to Nashville. I didn't know if she knew I was there and I wanted to stay longer but I knew she was in good hands with my mother and Dell on the case.

On the flight home, my body relaxed into the seat and I suddenly realized that I was exhausted, tired to my bones. Spending that much time in a hospital had drained me physically and emotionally. I couldn't stand being in hospitals, I tried to tell myself they were a place of healing, but I knew they were also places of heartache and misery. My days of putting doctors on pedestals were over, they were human and made mistakes every day, but I was especially thankful for the team of doctors at Pennsylvania Hospital that didn't give up on my sister and kept working to keep her heart beating more than once. They had brightened up my perspective on medical doctors once more.

Getting back on track wasn't easy when I got back, I had gotten behind in my classes and I had a ton of work that was waiting for me on the job. I called Philly at least twice a day and that curbed my worries about leaving and coming home. Talking to Helene was encouraging except when she told me that her heart was only beating at 25 percent capacity. That number just sounded low and scary to me.

***

My classes became a respite for me, a time when I could forget my regular life and think about how to solve the problems of the educational system. I was working hard in the statistical research class trying not to make the same mistakes I did in the previous semester. It became plain to me that the class was supposed to be a lesson of the last two chapters of a dissertation, the analysis and the conclusion. It wasn't just practicing with a set of variables to learn the software. I connected my questions to the statistics to prove my hypothesis.

The class that really galvanized my interest was the government and public policy for higher education class. I came face to face with the politics of education and how it affects minorities and poor people in a negative way. This was the direction that I wanted my research to go, where I thought I could make the most difference. I moved further away from the issues of the Lottery. You can't give an individual the desire to learn, that comes from within, but if you can clear the path for those persons who have financial issues or inadequate preparation to compete then you can have a positive impact on the numbers of students who can change their lives.

Helene was progressing well and would be moving to a rehabilitation facility soon. Cornelius and I made plans to drive up to Philly for a long weekend so that he and the girls could visit with her. We ran into monster traffic in Washington, DC that slowed us down so we drove directly to the hospital at around 9:00. She told us that she was going to be transferred to rehab the following day and I was so happy.

Rehabilitation was not easy for Helene, she needed both physical rehabilitation and mental rehabilitation, and sometimes they aren't moving forward in synch. They pushed her faster than she was ready to go maybe in both areas and she felt anxiety and chest pains. When they sent her to the emergency to check her heart they kept her. It was a disappointment to see her have another setback and have to go back to the hospital, we were so anxious to see her come home where the real healing begins.

We had only been back in Nashville a few weeks before my younger sister, Althea, called me and told me that she had been to the doctor and they said she had tumors on her kidney, pancreas, and spots on her lungs. They said it was stage four cancer. I was horrified and after I hung up I sat on the loveseat in my bedroom and started to cry hysterically. Why did my family have to suffer so much? I felt the cries as they scraped against my gut on the way up to my throat and I shook as the painful sounds were released. Cornelius looked at me from the bathroom across the room, saying nothing and unable to come towards me. Kim and Casey must have heard me over the television or their usual headphones because they both rushed into the room and put their arms around me. I could feel them rocking me and trying to comfort me saying, "Mama don't cry," without even knowing what was going on. I felt so blessed to have them at that moment as I tried to gather my emotions.

It was crystal clear that for whatever reasons Cornelius wasn't able to connect with me or comfort me and hadn't really been able to communicate intimately with me for all the years we had been together. I had told myself that I was a self-sufficient woman who could take care of my own pain and didn't need a shoulder to cry on, but it wasn't true. I was hurting, and this time I was glad I didn't have to keep pretending to be this superhuman being who pushes through everything like a machine on auto-pilot.

"Why us, why my family?" I asked. It seemed like we had more than our share of sickness. It was hard to think of my mother traveling up and down Broad Street from one hospital to another visiting my sisters. It seemed like so many others around us never had to suffer.

Pastor Drumwright preached about Job one Sunday and I had to admit that we were a blessed family and there's always plenty of suffering and hard times to go around. Drumwright reminded me if we weren't in a storm, then we had just come out of one or were about to go into one, and I knew he was right. I talked to Dell on the phone one day telling him how I felt like our family was being attacked and he put it all in perspective when he said, "We're all still here." So I shut down the pity party and got back into prayer. The Lord had never left me, but I must confess that as I got stronger and our schedules got busier, I didn't spend as much time in prayer and praise and it made me feel guilty.

Chapter Seventeen

Thank You, Jesus

Somehow with all the drama we made it through the holiday. Talking to Helene on New Year's Day, we vowed that 2008 would be a better year for us. It was a chaotic time and my whole family was taking it one day at a time. After a month Helene got out of the hospital and rehab and was at home doing well and Althea was taking an experimental chemotherapy that seemed to be working well to shrink her tumors.

I had by some miracle made four 'A's in my classes and I was ecstatic and ready to keep it going and registered for another twelve hours. I was taking another class from Dr. Hullette and when he returned one of my papers to me he said he recognized a fellow wordsmith and that made me feel great. When I was in high school I had dreams of someday being a writer, but I didn't feel I could make a living doing it.

Kim was performing in competitions with the half-timers and showed real talent and wanted to be an entertainer. I explained to her that it was a fine line to walk between following your dreams and having a way to pay the bills. We were both fortunate that I had my own interests to occupy me, which kept me from pressuring her to make the decisions that I would have preferred. It was a blessing not to have to live through my children, to allow them to make their own mistakes.

Kim was planning to go on the junior prom with some friends so we had a good time picking out dresses and shoes and hairstyles. The evening of the prom she looked great and I could see how she had grown up to be a very beautiful young woman. Cornelius took so many pictures and I teased her about letting him go with them. He said he would gladly go, and as he took more pictures of them he went all the way up the driveway to the car, and for a minute I thought he was going to climb in the car. It's hard watching your children grow up, and if you ever lose one you become overly protective of the others.

The spring semester was great, I learned a great deal and I finished up again with all 'A's. I realized that there was no challenge that I couldn't conquer if I worked hard. The girls also finished up a good year. We all deserved a break and I needed to see my sister so we planned to drive up to Philly at the end of May. It was good to be back in town and not have to be at the hospital. We picked up Helene and began to eat our way through the city. The Reading Terminal is where the eating begins. There is food from every nationality and ethnic group, and it's all delicious. I could see during our outing that Helene hadn't gotten all of her strength back. It was disturbing to see someone who had always been the epitome of strength and vitality weakened and short of breath, but she hung in there and it seemed like she got stronger with each day.

We visited Althea and she was doing very well, if you didn't know she was sick you would never have guessed it looking at her. By the time our week in town ended we had eaten our fill of cheese steaks, hot dogs, hoagies, pretzels, ice cream, water ice, cakes and pies, and gourmet chocolate. I drove home happy and content that both my sisters were in a good place health wise and I had partaken all of my favorite Philly foods.

When we got back home I got out my TSU graduate catalog. I had learned the hard way that it is not the number of hours you accumulate but the necessary classes that actually move you towards your degree. I found that I only lacked four classes before I would be concentrating solely on my dissertation and I got excited, however, during the summer session only two of the classes I needed were offered.

This summer was more laid back for me than I had experienced in a long time and it was right on time, I had been driving myself steadily for over three years. We took our yearly voyage to the ports of Belize, Honduras, and Freeport. It was fascinating to see that the poverty in other places in the world is not much different than that in the United States. Being in an academic environment provokes you to think and keeps your mind more aware of the common problems that confront our lives each day. You develop ideas about doing something that will change the world for good. I guess that's the purpose and why we encourage our youth to educate themselves for the benefit of the future for all of us.

At the close of the summer Kim started her senior year in high school, Casey began her last year of elementary school, and I registered for my last semester of regular classes. It was going to be a year of milestones for all of us. The fall semester with two classes was much easier compared to others when I was taking twelve hours. The timing worked out well with Kim having competitions and performances with the half-timer dance team. This was the special time in your life when you are preparing to go to college and cross over into adulthood. I knew what Kim had come through and I was proud to see her up on the stage dancing her heart out. It had made her more confidant and self-assured. Finding where our talent lies makes all the difference in how we feel about ourselves, and being the best at it is a tonic that revives the spirit.

The winding down of the courses in the doctoral program was just the beginning in a way. There was another comprehensive exam that had to be passed before you could move further to choosing a chairperson or advisor for your doctoral dissertation. We always heard about how many students were ABD, all but dissertations, and that wasn't a place I wanted to get trapped in. Preparation for the comprehensive exam was going to be more involved because there were twice the number of classes to study from. I had come so far that it didn't worry me, I had gained confidence with each successful semester. I knew what I had to do to pass, so I started reviewing and building my own study guide.

It was also time to choose my chairperson or mentor who would guide me through the dissertation process. I planned to ask Dr. Hullette, I knew that he would be hard but in the end I knew I would have a high quality paper. Unfortunately, when I did talk with him he said that he was contemplating retirement, his wife had been ill and he was having some health issues of his own. That took a lot of air out of my sail but he recommended I ask Dr. Fisher who had been demoted from Department Head. Dr. Hullette thought she had the experience with the process that I needed and that it might lift her spirits as well.

In that fall semester I did an internship at the Tennessee Higher Education Commission and I loved it. I got close to the movers and shakers who determined the policy and guidelines for the Tennessee Lottery HOPE scholarships. I was doing an interesting comparison between Tennessee and Kentucky, and who was doing the better job in higher education achievement and why. If I could have had it my way, I would have loved to work full time in this office, but it was one of those places where you have to be in the loop to join. I had the opportunity to attend a board meeting in the state capitol where they discussed the coming budget and a variety of issues on the agenda. This is the place where you could really make the changes that would positively affect the education opportunities for poor and minority students. Regrettably I didn't meet anyone who had the experience of being poor or a minority playing a part in the decision making.

***

The presidential election was front and center in most of our minds as it was discussed in my classes and with co-workers on the job. After the primary election I was stunned that Barack Obama had gotten the democratic nomination over Hilary

Clinton. Who knew the country was more ready for a black man in charge than a white woman. I will never forget the moment when the November election was called and Obama was declared the winner and the next president of the United States. It was a monumental moment, something that I had never realistically dreamed of seeing in my lifetime. Anyone who needed more proof that anything is possible would never be satisfied. True hope was restored for the country as well as for many of us personally.

The end of the year came quickly. They say time moves faster as you get older and that theory would get no argument from me. I ended my last semester of classes with an 'A' and a 'B', I wasn't happy about it but Dr. Boone have given me a 'B' on an internship on the master's level. He was one of those people who never gave 'A's, not even if you put a gun to his head. I didn't sweat it for long, I was done with all of my course work and that was amazing to me. I only had to write from this point on, except for the comprehensive exam in the spring. I had done a lot of work on my dissertation in the research for other classes during the last semesters so I was sure I had a jump on the program and would probably graduate in the spring. My only worry was that Kim would be graduating from high school in the spring and that was a special event in life and I didn't want her to have me in her spotlight.

The New Year 2009 started with a bang, I had great expectations for my family in this year and the inauguration of President Barack Obama was just the event to set the tone for so many positive things. I don't think I had ever watched the whole ceremony for any other president in my life, but I was fascinated and captivated by the whole thing. I saw it with my own eyes yet it was unbelievable to me. It was so wonderful to see this black family honored in this manner. For me, whenever something really good happens it scares me and I start to think something bad is going to spoil it. When Obama and Michelle walked on

Pennsylvania Avenue waving and thanking the people for making this moment possible I was so worried about their safety. I kept wishing they would get into the limo and stay protected, but I admired their fearlessness and courage to live their lives fully.

***

The spring was super busy and intense. Kim had to submit her college applications and she couldn't make up her mind where she wanted to go. I knew my child and she wasn't as mature or independent as she needed to be to go to a school far away from home. I encouraged her to apply to Tennessee State, it had been good enough for my father, good enough for me, countless other family members, and she would be close to home if there were any problems. She had been a big fan of the Tennessee State Aristocrat of Bands and I knew she would love to play in the marching band. There was also the added benefit of scholarships to apply for since she wouldn't be eligible for any financial aid. I kept on top of her grades with her teachers to help her stay above the 3.0 level.

The next thing on my agenda was to select the members of my dissertation committee and have an initial meeting with my chairperson. Dr. Fisher had agreed to serve as my advisor but after our first meeting I could tell that I was pretty much on my own. Contrary to Dr. Hullette's assumption that Dr. Fisher wanted to get back into the swing of things in the department, she was fully involved with her husband's preaching engagements and the gospel singing group that he traveled with. She was short on advice and guidance, so I pulled a few dissertations from Proquest to get more examples of how different dissertations were structured and flowed.

I wanted a diverse committee, so I chose two former instructors Dr. Glover, a close associate of Dr. Hullette, Dr. Jules, who was serving as the interim head of the department, and Dr. Ashford, a professor in the College of Public Service and Urban

Affairs as my outside member. I had two women and two men, two blacks and two whites. My committee members were going to be tough to satisfy, I had chosen individuals who would make sure I had the highest quality dissertation possible. I would have loved to have Dr. Hullette's constructive criticism to get me prepared, but we all have to make adjustments along the way.

The first three chapters of the dissertation had to be approved by the committee before you could technically go further in your writing, but I had finished most of the five chapters. I decided to send Dr. Fisher the first three chapters of my dissertation which was titled: "State Policies for Higher Education: Which are the most effective in raising enrollment levels?" to critique before I distributed copies to the other members of my committee.

My first meeting with Dr. Fisher was nonproductive. I could tell that she hadn't read any of my paper. However, she suggested a few things that I should be sure about before I submit my paper for evaluation. The semester was passing quickly so I worked on polishing up my paper and scheduled a date for my proposal. I met again with Dr. Fisher and that time it did seem like she had at least skimmed over it. She still didn't offer me any feedback, positive or negative, but I felt like I had put together a good paper, so I made four copies and delivered them to my committee members three weeks before my proposal date. I prepared a power-point presentation over the three chapters and started practicing.

The day of my dissertation proposal I wasn't sure which suit I wanted to wear. I thought about it being just the proposal and not my final defense so I decided not to get too fancy. I wore a casual beige linen suit that I had gotten on sale at JC Penney. I was pretty confident. I had practiced going through my power-point and felt comfortable discussing my research.

My presentation was about 20 minutes, and then the barrage of questions was launched. I hadn't expected the amount of criticism I got from Dr. Glover and Dr. Jules. They both expressed that my subject matter was much too broad and I would never be able to finish the research. After taking a few more hits on the proposal, Dr. Fisher asked me if I would step outside in the halfway while they had their discussion. Sitting in the hallway I was glad there were no other students around, I had been blown away in there. I had worked so hard and now I didn't know what the outcome would be. After about fifteen minutes, Dr. Fisher came out and told me that the committee didn't vote to pass me, that they felt that I needed to focus my research on one specific problem and clearly state the purpose.

I returned to the room embarrassed that I thought I had been ready. I remembered the wise warning from Dr. Poland in the calculus class, "Don't go and get all cocky thinking that I got this." Maybe I had gotten cocky, thinking that I could solve all the problems of higher education in my dissertation. I thanked my committee members and they gave me the copies of my proposal back with their corrections on it. Then it was only Dr. Fisher and I in the room.

"Did I fail on my proposal?" I asked her timidly, not really wanting to hear her answer.

"You need to give the committee members what they want," she said nonchalantly.

"What was that supposed to mean?" I thought.

Feeling dejected, I gathered up my corrected chapters and walked out to my car. When I got home I told Cornelius that I didn't pass, but I wasn't quite sure it was a failure. He told me not to sweat it, just regroup, make the corrections and try again. That was easy for him to say, each semester of writing was costing me over a thousand dollars and my Sallie Mae money had run out long ago. Then again, there really weren't any other choices, besides I hadn't come this far to end up ABD.

At least Kimberly didn't have to worry about sharing the spotlight with me in May, there was no way I was graduating in a few months. I narrowed my dissertation from the equity and fairness of financial aid awarded by merit versus need to the evaluation of the efficiency of financial aid awarded by merit versus need. I painstakingly made the corrections page by page that Dr. Glover and Dr. Jules specified on the first draft. I decided that I would meet with each committee member one-on-one to really understand what they were looking for in my paper. Dr. Ashford was the most helpful. She gave me several suggestions for a theoretical framework to build the paper around. She also gave me a book that explained the theory of efficiency. Dr. Glover gave me some excerpts from his own dissertation on accurately stating the problem and Dr. Jules gave me a few points to consider, so I took it all in and went to work rewriting my second draft.

***

In the meantime we got good news, Kim was accepted to TSU which wasn't a great surprise, but she also got an academic scholarship to cover her tuition and that was music to our ears. It was important to me that she have the full college experience which included living on campus and not having to worry about finances like I did. While I was re-writing I wanted to stay relaxed and not put more pressure on myself, so I took some time to enjoy the end of Kim's senior year and the high school activities. I enjoyed going with her to take her high school pictures and preparing for the senior prom. It was during times like these that I was more aware of the high school experiences that I didn't get to share with Courtney, picking out a dress and fussing about how high the heels were on the shoes, and the pluses of wearing a slip when no one wears them anymore.

The end of Kim's senior year came quickly and seeing her in that white cap and gown thrilled me, and to think she was graduating with honors, who knew. At the end of the ceremony I watched her as she said so many goodbyes and gave so many farewell hugs knowing how precious this moment was. Even when most of the graduates had gone home, she still lingered to speak to a yet another fellow student. I could see she didn't want to leave this time of her life, the close of a chapter, and was delaying it in every way she could. I finally told Cornelius to go over and tell her it was time to go.

A week later I made an appointment for her to audition for the TSU marching band. Kim was the queen of procrastination and for months I had been asking her if she was ready and she kept telling me not yet. Well school had ended and it was now or never. On the way to campus she was nervous because she had not prepared herself for the audition. I figured that whatever happened it would be a learning experience, if she did fine it would increase her self-confidence, if she did badly she would know that she needed to practice and raise her game. I listened outside while she and some other last minute students warmed up before their turn. I couldn't hear her play, but when she came out she was all smiles, she had made the band.

Chapter Eighteen

Keeping the Faith

We all needed a break and I was worried about how my sisters were doing so we decided to take another trip to Philly. While we were there, Cornelius and I, Kim, Casey, Helene and her daughter, and my mother were all inseparable. Our first outing was at the Art Museum, next the outside market on South Ninth Street, the Reading Terminal, King of Prussia Mall, and finally Atlantic City. Helene seemed to get stronger and more confident with each day of running around town. It felt good to see her on her on her feet again.

One afternoon we all went to Althea's for a cookout. Al was doing well and appeared fine except she was very thin, an unhealthy thin. I had never seen her anywhere near that size in her entire life and my thoughts drifted to the possibility of life without my little sister. I cleared my mind scared that if I let those thoughts linger that they might become real. I left town feeling better for having spent the time, but I knew that none of us was at the point we wanted to be.

By the time we got back to Nashville I felt like I could sleep for a week. We had two weeks before Kim would be moving on campus for a summer program that provided some enrichment classes for students with science, technology, engineering, or math majors. She also got an invitation to come to the marching band camp at the end of the summer. I remembered when I first moved on campus in Pittsburgh before I transferred to Nashville and knew the long list of clothing and supplies backwards.

On move-in day as Cornelius and Kim loaded up the truck it hit me that Kim was going to college, technically she was leaving home. I was happy for her to have the chance to become more independent out on her own. After Kim got her dorm room assignment we met her roommate and put her things away. I made the bed while Cornelius hooked up the TV to the cable. It was when we got home that I worried if Casey would be lonesome and how long it would take both of them to get adjusted.

***

In the summer I registered again to continue working on my proposal. My spring semester grades came out and I had an incomplete on the dissertation class. Dr. Fisher said that I didn't need to present my proposal again if I could get my committee members to sign my new draft. I started with Dr. Ashford, I had taken her recommendation of focusing on the efficiency as the basis in which financial aid should be distributed. I was using the theoretical framework for efficiency that was in the literature she had given me. I gave her my revised version of the proposal and arranged to come back in about a week.

Dr. Ashford was satisfied with the revision and signed off on my proposal. I must say that she was one of the most gracious people that I had come in contact with during all my years at TSU. She was always welcoming and made me feel like I was one of the most special people on earth. Every e-mail sent by her always made me smile. If I ever am in the position to guide or lead I will certainly follow her example.

Dr. Glover was next on my hit list, he had emphasized the need for a conceptual framework that organized the paper and helped it flow. When I got to his office, he was only concerned with reading that section, so instead of taking the revised copy, he read it while I sat in his office and then he signed off. I was definitely feeling more positive about getting through the proposal during the summer semester. Dr. Jules would be the hardest, mainly because he was so busy serving as department head. I dropped a copy of the revised version of the proposal with his secretary and went home to wait patiently.

***

When the STEM program ended it was time for band camp to begin. Kim was so excited because she had seen the TSU Aristocrat of Bands all of her life at the TSU homecoming parades. Parents were asked to come to the orientation for band members. We were advised to let them be adults, leave them alone and not coddle them. The students were told to remember why they were there, it's all about completing their education.

Each student had to go through the ritual that I knew so well, go on stage and introduce themselves. Kim went up and didn't appear to be as nervous as I probably would have been and I was glad about that. They told us their rules and regulations for practice and conduct when they were traveling. Dr. Graves the head director said that one thing they did not tolerate was hazing. That was a little puzzling to me because I didn't see how that would apply to a band, but it was comforting to know they ran a tight and disciplined ship.

We moved all of her things into the new dorm, met her new roommate, and gave Kim a hug goodbye. We were all excited and proud that she had the opportunity to be a part of something that was held in high esteem at TSU. Cornelius and I laughed all the way home with the thought that we would have to do this again in two more weeks at the freshman dorm.

I spent the rest of the evening working on my dissertation. Most of the statistical questions were the same, but I had added a few more to address the efficiency of aid awards. Around 10:00 I decided to call it a night, but before I had time to shut down the computer Kim called and wanted me to come back to campus.

"What's going on?" I asked.

"I'll tell you when you get here," she said mysteriously.

"Okay," I said, "I'll send your Daddy and Casey over there." I was tired and didn't feel like driving.

"No, Mama, I only want you to come," she said, "Just you."

"All right, I'm on my way," I told her.

Suddenly I began to worry, what was wrong, what had happened? My imagination started running away with me with wild guesses.

"Stop," I said to myself. Wait until you get there before you start tripping.

I told Cornelius about the phone call and made the short drive again back to campus. When I pulled into the parking lot of the dorm where the band members were staying I could see Kim standing on the steps outside waiting. I parked and walked over to meet her as she came down the steps. Before I could ask any questions she put her arms around me in a hug like she was holding on for her life and began to cry. I just hugged her back and we stood there for about five minutes as she cried her heart out. I was stunned, she had only been here one day, what was wrong? All I could do was stand there quietly and wait while she emptied out whatever was hurting her inside. When she was done I asked her what had happened.

"Mama, I didn't know it was going to be like this," she said through her tears.

"What happened?" I asked again, "Did somebody hurt you?"

I thought about the hazing comment from Dr. Graves.

"Mama, they called me so many names that I have never been called before," she said.

"Who did, Kim?" I asked.

She said the upper class band members cursed them out and down talked them and called them names.

"What names, what did they say?" I kept asking her.

Kim kept shaking her head not wanting to tell me the words. So I starting guessing, "Did they call you a bitch or nigger?"

"Yeah they did, but I've been called those before, that don't bother me, they called us other things worse."

"What, did they call you a ho?" I asked.

"Yeah they did but they said other things worse."

I left the guessing game alone after that, I couldn't possibly guess what craziness some of these ghetto minded students had twisted their mouths to say. I just hugged her.

"The world is full of mean people who will do whatever they can to try and humiliate you and bring you down," I told her, holding her tight. "You have to know who you are." She nodded her head against me. "You are Kim Brown and you are none of the names they have called you. Let those things roll off your back because they have nothing to do with you."

She gathered her emotions and was calm.

Then I asked her, "Do you want me to report what happened to the director?"

"No, Mama, that will just make it worse," she said, "I just feel like quitting."

"If you don't want to do this then quit," I said, "But don't let anyone else make you quit, you have as much right to be here as anyone else."

She told me that she had refused to breakdown in front of them and then I knew they had said everything they could think of to try and weaken her resolve.

"I'm proud of you," I said, "We Browns always hold on to our pride and dignity."

I asked her a few more questions to make sure that she had not been singled-out or treated differently than any of the other freshman. Then I started singing our old theme song, "We are survivors, we not gonna give up, we gonna work harder cause we surviving," and she started laughing and I knew she would get through the night.

On the drive home I thought about how no matter how hard you try and no matter what you do, you can't protect your children from the hardships of this world. You can't follow them around and remove every obstacle. You can only be there for them and support them as they go through the many challenges that none of us can escape. I had done for my children what my parents had done for me, taught them to pray and call on the name of Jesus to help you fight the many battles that are almost guaranteed. I was sorry that Kim had to go through this experience; black people should have learned to treat each other better by now. I thought that Kim would have avoided some of this by attending a HBCU but I guess I was wrong, human nature is human nature and it's not always good. I prayed for her strength and for a hedge of protection to surround her, and I planned to e-mail Dr. Graves first thing in the morning.

    Cornelius couldn't wait to hear what happened when I got home. I explained that the band was hazing the freshman, putting them through their own initiation process. He told me about the things that he had gone through when he was freshman on the football team in college and how that's a part of it. Cornelius said that she's strong enough to handle that as long as they don't put their hands on her. I listened unwilling to expend the energy to tell a man that sometimes words hurt more, deeper, and longer than if someone was to hit you. Casey even got riled up saying if anybody does something to Kim she was going to hurt them.

    There were other days during band camp that Kim called home saying she wanted to quit. The hazing was rough and the days and nights of practicing in the heat with the mosquitoes was just as bad. She said that a few of the other freshman had quit saying it wasn't worth it. We talked and I encouraged her and asked if she wanted me to come over and put a stop to it. She always said no, and somehow she hung in there.

***

    I spent the last weeks of the summer session trying to get Dr. Jules to sign-off on my proposal. The first draft I left with the secretary had been lost or misplaced and I had to leave another one. A few times when I showed up for our meeting he had something more pressing to tend to. When we finally met he had marked a few corrections that I needed to make, but he signed-off with the understanding that I would get them done.

Alleluia, I had finally gotten the first three chapters of my dissertation finished before the summer semester ended. The proposal and defense cannot be done in the same semester. Hopefully I would only have to register for one more semester to complete it and defend it before my committee.

I had learned a lot from my unfortunate dissertation proposal experience. I made appointments to meet with my committee members before I did my final draft. I wanted to find out what they would be looking for before I sent them a draft. I saw Carol, one of my cohorts, coming out of Dr. Fisher's office when I came for our meeting to discuss where I was in my writing. I wondered how the process was going for her and if she felt like she was getting the mentoring she needed. I caught up with her and we talked for a minute but I didn't get a chance to ask her what she thought about Dr. Fisher. She was angry and upset and vented that no one had told her that our papers need to be theoretically based. There was no need to say anything more.

In my meeting with Dr. Fisher, she didn't have any requirements for my final draft, her mind was already operating in another place and it didn't have anything to do with my dissertation. I knew if I got my committee on board then the paper was good enough for her.

At the start of the fall semester I met with Dr. Ashford first. She was no nonsense and very straightforward in what she was looking for in my statistics and conclusion. I had basically satisfied her when I changed the theoretical framework so she said no other recommendations. I dropped off copies of the last two chapters with Dr. Glover and Dr. Jules and decided to give them a couple of weeks to read it before I came back for corrections. I thought it would give me a chance to catch my breath and relax since our schedule had really lightened up with Kim out of high school and the extra-curricular activities she participated in.

Casey had finished her swimming lessons and had joined

the NAC swim team but it was much less hectic. However, just because Kim stayed on campus didn't mean she wasn't going to keep us busy. The band schedule was running her ragged. They practiced from 5:00 in the afternoon to around midnight every day and most of the day on the weekend and she was overwhelmed with her classes. This semester was primetime for bands at HBCU's and the competition was fierce.

    I thought about my freshman year at Carnegie-Mellon in Pittsburgh and how I had needed help from my brother Dell. He decided to let me sink or swim, and I sank. I also thought about what the band directors advised, to treat them as responsible adults. I had the choice to sit back and watch her fail and lose her scholarship and then give her some advice, or get in there with her and give her time to make the necessary adjustments to make it on her own with her scholarship in place. I chose the latter. I must say that I do believe in tough love, but having been on the other side of the coin I was determined to help her as much as I could.

    I picked Kim up from TSU and brought her to my job where we studied and worked on her Chemistry homework problems. I finished one of her English papers to keep it from being late. I typed the notes that she had to turn in for her wellness class. I did whatever it took to keep her in the game. I didn't know if I was making the right decision or not, but I refused to stand back and watch her drown.

Chapter Nineteen

To God be the Glory

As a proud TSU alumnus and doctoral candidate it was a great moment to see Kim marching out on the field as a member of the Aristocrat of Bands. Cornelius was about to burst inside with pride as he videotaped every minute they were on the field. I was so happy for her because I knew what it took for her to get to this day. Later that evening I asked her if it was worth it, all the verbal abuse she had suffered, all the late practices, the aching feet and swollen lips, and she said it was worth it. It was amazing. I got a little choked up because I knew that feeling, paying the high price of hard work to reach your goal, and the sense of accomplishment and satisfaction that comes from a job well done.

It was a special time for me when Kim and I were at TSU at the same time. Once on my way to the library I saw her walking toward the Performance Arts building with some other band members going to practice and I felt blessed to be able to see her doing her thing. I was proud that she had the courage to stick it out. As Pastor Drumwright had said on many occasions; she had tied a knot and held on.

The next week I picked up the last two chapters of my dissertation from Dr. Glover and was pleasantly surprised that there were no major corrections to be made. I was on a roll. Now I only needed to speak with Dr. Jules, but he was hard to catch, he was wearing about three hats in the department and that kept him on the run. When I finally got to meet with him he hadn't had time to go over the chapters. Feeling sympathetic because of the many times I had tried to see him, Dr. Jules took some time and read the chapters while I was in his office. I was in his research statistics class so I knew that was where he would focus his attention. I looked around his office while he read, looking at pictures of his wife and son, a flag from his native country, books, certificates, and piles of papers.

When he was done Dr. Jules told me that I needed to add some additional tables showing the demographics of the states but other than that it looked good and I was so surprised not to get much opposition that it made me nervous. I began to wonder if I had pulled everything together or were they just waiting to ambush me at my defense. I decided to stay positive, I had worked really hard on it and in my mind it was an excellent paper.

I spent a week editing my own paper before I started the power-point presentation. It was mid-October before I had finally finished my presentation. With that done I went to Kinko's to make five copies of the final draft of my dissertation to give to my committee members. When I met with Dr. Fisher to give her the final draft she told me to choose a tentative date for my defense and send it to the other members of the committee. It took a bit of finagling to find the date but it was finally scheduled for November 9 at 1:00 in the afternoon.

I spent a lot of time reading my paper and practicing my presentation. I had been told the presentation should be about 40 minutes. I have a tendency to talk fast when I get nervous, so I focused on talking slower because I didn't want my power-point to run short. I scheduled a hair appointment and put my navy blue Austin Reed suit in the cleaners. I wanted to be polished in my defense and my appearance.

I took the day off work on the morning of my defense so I could keep the day as stress free as possible. I went over my presentation once more after breakfast. Then I spent the rest of the morning trying to stay relaxed. I felt like the butterflies in my stomach were having Olympic game tryouts. I started to get dressed early so I could do it in stages and not get flustered or sweaty. I made an emergency copy of my power-point on a CD as a backup just in case something went wrong with my jump drive.

My dissertation defense was on the downtown campus which was a little farther than the main campus so I left the house about forty-five minutes early so I could drive slowly and have time to gather my nerves. Fifteen minutes before the hour I put some mints in my mouth and walked in the building. I was looking quite sharp so I got a few looks as I came into the building and walked through the hallway, and it boosted my confidence. Dr. Fisher had already called the IT department and the presentation equipment was already set up in the conference room. I loaded my jump drive on the computer and sat down to concentrate on breathing deeply from my diaphragm until my committee members arrived.

When everyone was present and we had exchanged greetings Dr. Fisher told me I could begin. I stood up and thanked everyone for their help and assistance on my project and started the slide show. I went through the presentation just as I had practiced, using my own words and reading from the slide and it felt natural. This was my research and I knew what I was talking about. I was the authority on my subject. When I came to the end. I was ready for their questions. The grilling session wasn't bad, I didn't have any problem with any of the questions. When there were no more questions Dr. Fisher asked me to wait outside. I was relieved that I had gotten through the defense smoothly. It was about fifteen minutes later when Dr. Fisher came out and asked me to come back into the conference room.

I came into the room and Dr. Fisher said, "May I be the first to introduce Dr. Karen Sloan-Brown."

"Oh, thank you," I said sincerely as I looked at each member.

I was so happy. Dr. Glover and Dr. Jules both shook my hand on their way out and congratulated me.

Dr. Ashford took my hand and said, "That's comparable to the dissertations we have in our department, congratulations."

I can barely describe the moment, it was over the moon for me.

"You did it," Dr. Fisher said as we left the room.

"Thank you so much for everything," I said, brimming with joy.

All the way home I just thanked the Lord for bringing me on this journey and carrying me through. "Dr. Karen Sloan-Brown," I said aloud, who would have thought it. I hadn't told anyone except for Cornelius that I was defending that day. I didn't want to have to explain or talk about it if things didn't go well. I called Cornelius to tell him that I had finished and that I had passed.

"That's great, Karen, I'm happy for you, congratulations."

He wanted the details of how things went and I told him I'd tell him later. I barely had time to get to Casey's school to pick her up. Now I had to think of a way to celebrate. I called Helene to tell her the news and she said she was definitely coming down again for my graduation. I walked on air for about a week until I realized that the deadline to submit my dissertation to the graduate school was fast approaching and I had just become aware of the specifications for submission. I had to adjust all of my margins, add another section for graphs and figures, and a host of other changes.

I rushed through the process of getting my committee members' signatures on the final copy with the correct weight of paper. When I walked into the graduate school office with my final papers and signed them in I knew that I was finally finished. I had earned the terminal degree. By this time I had considered myself a lifelong learner and enjoyed the pursuit of knowledge. I loved the feeling of growing and expanding my mind and I really didn't want that to end, but there were no more degrees to aspire to. My years at TSU had come to a close.

I had already ordered my cap and gown, but now an exit interview was a requirement for graduation so I headed to the Student Union Building to get it done. In the interview they were asking me my plans and goals after graduation, where I planned to work, and all I could think of is that I have already done all those things. I didn't know what my plans were. I felt like I had followed a path set before me and I didn't know where it led. I just wanted to enjoy this moment and reflect on the experiences that brought me to this point. Yet, whenever I told anyone that I had successfully defended my dissertation they would ask me what I was going to do. I stopped mentioning it because I felt uncomfortable not having an answer or why I had pursued this degree.

***

I got more excited by the day, Helene was flying in and my brother Dell from California would also be coming for the ceremony. A December graduation is hectic, because it falls in the middle of Christmas shopping and decorating, but with out-of-town company my to-do list was getting longer by the minute. I invited my neighbors and my aunts to come over after the graduation. Remembering my previous graduation I didn't expect them all to come, but I still wanted the house to look nice and have plenty of food. We all worked together to get some quick cleaning done and get the Christmas decorations up and the lights hung outside. I couldn't settle down enough to prepare anything so I ordered party platters from Publix.

I picked up my cap and gown from the bookstore and it came with the doctoral hood and the velvet down the front and on the sleeves of the gown and it struck me again, I would be Dr. Karen Sloan-Brown. Sitting under the dryer at the beauty shop my mind wandered back to the day that I walked the 72 steps up that steep hill to my car and pleaded to the Lord to make a way out of no way for me. From that day my life changed and has been evolving ever since. On that day I never dreamed that I would have come to this place in my life.

On Friday, Dell and Helene had been picked up from the airport and were settling in at the house before it was time for me to go to the practice run-through of the ceremony. I knew the drill for the graduation rehearsal and not even Dr. Lockheed threats about behavior during the graduation service could subdue the feelings I had when I sat in the Gentry before the graduates lined up. This was truly a great accomplishment for me. Ph.D and Ed.D graduates were told to go to the front of the line.

When we went through our practice run I realized that I would be seated in the front row. "Wow," I thought to myself, I definitely had come a long way. Dr. Lockheed explained that doctoral graduates would take their hoods up to the stage and then it would be placed on us by the Dean. I couldn't wait to tell everybody that I would be front and center.

The next morning Cornelius dropped me off at the front. This day was so special I had bought new shoes and worn a skirt for the occasion. Standing near the front of the graduation line, there was only one person in front of me on the left of a double line, a tall distinguished black man who would lead us all in. The doctoral graduates were told not to put their hoods on, that we should drape them over our left arm until we were hooded. Just before the graduation was to begin I saw Helene and Dell come in with my mother and we waved to each other. Dell is characteristically late so I figured that Cornelius and the girls had gone ahead in the truck and left them the car.

I felt like I could fly when I heard the "Pomp and Circumstance" begin. I wished my Dad could be here to see this day. I wished that Courtney would have had the chance to experience this feeling. I marched slow and deliberately wanting this moment to last as long as possible. This must be what a Rock star feels like when they come out on stage, looking at the crowd while they look at you. I felt so special standing at the front row while the rest of the graduates continued to march in. I saw some of my professors sitting in the faculty section and Dr. Ashford even waved to me and a few others nodded. This moment was priceless.

I found my family and I waved and I could see them taking videos and pictures. Diplomas were given beginning with the undergraduate degrees, but I wasn't anxious, I wanted to sit in that seat as long as I could. When the doctorate graduates were asked to stand there were eleven of us and we walked over to the stage. I watched as each graduate was hooded and I felt a kindred spirit with them all knowing the hard work that it took to get to this day.

When I heard my name called I walked up the stairs and over to the Dean with my pride and dignity intact and accepted my diploma. One lifted the hood from my arm and adjusted the folds. The other Dean took one end and I tilted my head back so they could place it over my head and around my neck. One adjusted it to hang properly in the back and I could see flashes going off in front of me. I walked over to the president to shake his hand and posed for another picture. I walked to my seat and remained standing until the last Ph.D graduate was hooded.

All the graduates were asked to stand and then the audience applauded. A few words were said and then we marched out leading the December 2009 graduating class of TSU. Cornelius and the girls found me and we took more pictures inside and outside of the Gentry Center. We found Dell, my Mother and Helene, who couldn't climb the stairs and I floated home.

Cornelius gave me a bracelet with black diamonds as a graduation gift. It had been a beautiful day. Nevertheless, I was in a family of all chiefs and no Indians, so I had to neaten up the house, chill the champagne, and go pick up the trays for my celebration party before 5:00 when my family would arrive.

When no one offered to ride with me to help I knew not much had changed and the aura of the morning was beginning to fade.

I made it back to the house and recruited Dell to make some punch while I changed my clothes. My Aunt Carolyn came right on time and brought a cake that lifted my spirits right back into the clouds. It was in the university colors of blue and white with the TSU emblem and a woman wearing a cap and gown jumping for joy with the words, "There's a Doctor in the House." I just loved it and had Cornelius take a picture of it.

I was surprised and touched when all of my aunts and uncles, cousins and their significant others, and even some of my neighbors came with congratulations to share this occasion with me.

My uncle Frank pulled me to the side and said, "The one thing about education, once you have it, nobody can take it away from you."

We ate and ate, and Cornelius made a toast and we drank champagne. Even some of my family who I didn't think touched alcohol anymore had a sip.

It was a great evening. The kids had made up a dance, and Kim and I danced together. We all even watched a DVD of a Sade concert. I couldn't have asked for a better way to celebrate my graduation. It was a great opportunity for family to get together and fellowship with one another. In hard times we drift away from socializing and spending time together as we deal with our individual situations. Throughout the evening I could not count how many times I was asked what I was going to do now, what were my plans, was I going to change jobs? I put off the questions saying, "I'm just going to rest for a while" or "there are several things I'd like to do, but I haven't decided."

The questions weighed on my mind over the next few weeks of the holiday season. I had always taken this opportunity as a journey, a path laid out for me by God. I hadn't given much thought as to whether this was the end or the beginning, I had no idea. I had faith that the final destination would be revealed to me at the appropriate time. What if this experience was only about the journey and there wasn't anything else? What if this was simply a healing for me, a period of growth, something that showed me life is worth living and it moves on and keeps on in the face of a multitude of circumstances? I could accept that because that in itself was a lot to me, definitely worth the trip.

However, I felt the pressure from co-workers, friends, and family to provide a justification for earning the degrees. I started to feel like I had something else to prove, that I needed to show people more evidence of my success. I needed to get a higher paying job, or I needed to buy an expensive car to show my achievement was worth it.

I started out the year applying for teaching positions at TSU, MTSU, Vanderbilt, and even got desperate enough to apply at the University of Phoenix. I didn't have any real teaching experience so they were all long shots. I even reconsidered teaching with Metro but it wasn't something I wanted to do, it was more that I felt I had to do it for appearances. I applied for several administrative positions on the Meharry jobs website that I really didn't want, but it would seem like a step up. I even applied with the Tennessee Higher Education Commission.

I had reached the echelon of where it's not what you know but who you know and I didn't know anyone. It was about three months into the year before I even got an interview, and it was over the phone. That went well enough that they wanted me to come in person. I had also received another call so both interviews were at Meharry as Program Coordinators. I really wanted to make a good impression so I went to the Brooks Brothers Outlet at Opry Mills Mall and bought myself a gray pinstripe power suit and tailored shirt to match. As usual I thought both interviews went well and we talked in great detail about the responsibilities of the positions and then I never heard a word from either one.

How could I have accomplished this much and still feel like a failure. I submitted a couple of manuscripts to a few journals and they always recommended I try another journal. I decided to try and write some grants to pursue my own research which was what I really wanted to do, but I didn't get any awarded. I wasn't sure what the problem was but I felt like I needed a mentor, someone who could give me some guidance and constructive criticism in building my new career. I wrote some letters to the Education Policy Department at Vanderbilt, but I didn't find any takers.

I was starting to get a bit frustrated and would spend a lot of time pondering over the challenges of a black person trying to move forward. I thought about the struggles of my own father who I considered to be a much better person than I was. I started questioning what had gone wrong, why was it so hard to make progress, to find that open door. It was then I made up my mind that I would write a book about it to occupy my mind while I continued to look for a job. I started it as a small project, but with each sentence it grew larger and my view expanded until I was writing a review of black people over the last 100 years. As I got further into the research I realized it was too extensive for me to complete.

One morning at work I got an e-mail my neighbor, Bonita, sent me about the 9/11 tragedy. It was a short film about how small factors made the difference between life and death for so many people. The inability to find keys, the missing of a subway, or the elevator taking too long saved the lives of countless individuals. The essence of the e-mail was that we are where we are supposed to be. I pondered that thought and then I embraced it. We all need to live in the present and in the now, it is what we are supposed to be doing. Sure there may be some profound destiny that we are moving towards but each day is not happenstance, it is designated.

The book I was working on began to consume me and I realized that writing it was what I was supposed to be doing. I labored on the book which I call "A Reflection: What a

Difference a Day Makes, What About 100 Years" for nearly two years before I finished it. Now I hope I'll find someone who wants to publish it. I see it as an expression of who I am as a black person and where I have come from in my journey. I hope it will motivate others to live up to their full potential. The research and writing in earning the degrees gave me the confidence and experience to come back to what I initially wanted to do, be a writer. The path had brought me full circle, to an early dream of writing, and now I truly had something to say.

    I wanted to share my experiences and be the encouragement to others that so many had been for me. I had learned more about myself than anything I may have learned in a book. I found that many of the limits that we encounter, the boundaries that hinder our successes are the ones that we have place upon ourselves. I had discovered my hidden potential, my inner strength, and the will to persevere. I rediscovered some lost talents and abilities, allowed myself to dream once more, learned patience, acceptance of myself as well as others. I learned that life is bittersweet with events that are so bitter they choke off our breath and then there are the sweet moments that make it all worth the living. So no matter what we go through or what knocks us off our feet, we can recover, we are resilient if we allow ourselves the chance to bounce back. I had suffered through one of the greatest hurts in life, the loss of a child, and I found joy again, I found peace again, I found hope again.

    None of this means that I am exempt from the heartbreaks and heartaches in my personal relationships or the abundance of disappointments that come with working towards my goals in life. It simply means that I can survive the everyday and the unusual drama. It means that the Lord has blessed me with His mercy and grace and I am most grateful. James Cleveland said it best in his gospel song, *"I don't feel no ways tired, I've come too far from where I started from. Nobody told me that the road would be easy, I don't believe He brought me this far to leave me."*

www.ingramcontent.com/pod-product-compliance
Lightning Source LLC
Chambersburg PA
CBHW070608300426
44113CB00010B/1456